INSTANT POT
COOKBOOK FOR BABIES

The Complete Baby Food Cookbook with Delicious and Nutritious Instant Pot Recipes For Your Baby and Toddler

Diana Dilan

Warning-Disclaimer

Contents

12 – 18 MONTHS

18 MONTHS – 3 YEARS

Introduction

Introducing solids to your little one can be an exciting, nerve-wracking journey. There are no rules, while at the same time there are many. You can trust your gut, but not completely. You should pay attention to what your baby is telling you, but also know when to disregard them.

If you are a parent and are confused, welcome to the club. We have all been in your shoes and have been through that bumpy ride. The secret to success is always patience, strong will, and excellent knowledge. I may not be able to help you convince your baby to eat that yummy carrot puree, but I can surely help you by offering great knowledge that will ensure that your little one will be healthy and eat nothing but the most nutritious foods.

Inside these pages you will find:

- Everything you need to know about how and when to introduce solid foods
- Why and how the IP will help you on that journey
- The ultimate cooking chart for the foods for the whole first year
- A sample schedule for solid food introduction to get you started
- The healthiest foods you should start with
- The most common allergens and how to recognize allergy reactions
- The complete month-to-month ingredient list
- 100 delicious and nutritious Instant Pot Baby and Toddler Recipes

Own an Instant Pot? You have nothing to worry about. Let this book and your extraordinary appliance set your baby on a path of healthy progress.

The First Feeding and Beyond

Congratulations! Your bundle of joy is ready for solid foods and exploring new tastes and flavors. This must be a very exciting period for you; however, it can also be just as nerve-racking. Do you start at four or six months? Should you start with veggies or fruits? Do you really need to feed your baby single-ingredient purees the first month? What to do if your baby refuses to eat? How to know if they are full? Introducing solids can really be a confusing, and for some overwhelming, journey. Why? Because there really are no rules.

If you have researched this subject a bit, you are probably familiar with the fact that there are tons of conflicting theories online. In fact, visit two pediatricians and you will most likely get different advice. But, as confusing as this may be, don't worry, you will do just fine. After all, mamma knows best. Just trust your gut, and most importantly, listen to your baby.

WHEN TO START?

Like I said, there are no rules. While some babies may be ready to indulge in yummy potato purees at four months, others may need to wait a month or two more. It all depends on your baby's unique needs and the progress they have made so far. Although you should consult with your pediatrician when to start introducing solids, most babies are ready to taste real foods at four-six months. Here are some signs that indicate your little one will accept food well:

- Sitting well when supported
- The "extrusion reflex" is fading (not pushing food out of their mouth but using the tongue to swallow it)
- Curious about food – eyeing and trying to reach food
- Noticeable weight gain – if the baby has twice the weight since birth weight and is at least four months old
- The baby has great head control

WHAT TO START WITH?

This also depends on your baby, whether it is breastfed or not, the progress they have made since birth, etc. This should be established after a talk with your pediatrician, who can advise you accordingly.

For many years it was believed that offering bland cereals as a first meal was the best introduction to solids. However, this is no longer something most pediatricians agree with because there is no real evidence this offers health benefits or other advantages.

Most agree the first solid food you should introduce your baby to should be avocado or sweet potato. You can also choose banana, but keep in mind that banana and all fruits (except avocados) have a sweet, pleasant taste. It will be harder to transition from bananas to carrots than, for instance, from avocados to carrots, because your little one will expect all foods to taste just as sweet as the banana.

If you are starting at six months and your baby is breastfed, your doctor may even recommend you start with meat instead, although most agree that the first food should be plant-based.

In short, it is entirely up to you and your doctor. There are no wrong or right choices as long as the baby's health is the number one priority.

HOW TO DO IT?

The only rule to introducing solids to babies is to do it gradually, one ingredient at a time. There is some confusion wrapped around this one too, but keep in mind that the gradual approach is the safest one. You should offer the same single-ingredient puree for three days before introducing a new type of food. This gives you plenty of time to monitor your baby and see if they are showing signs of an allergic reaction. If your baby is allergic to something, the gradual approach will help you pinpoint exactly what food the baby is allergic to and spare your baby the inconvenience of testing for allergens.

Okay, but how do you actually feed your baby? The traditional – and most convenient approach – is to start by spoon-feeding your infant thin, runny purees and cereals.

For the first feeding, give your baby no more than a couple of teaspoons (two should be quite enough) of a single-ingredient puree. Make sure you use a plastic spoon with a soft tip to prevent gum injuries. Do not fill the whole spoon, but put a small amount of the puree on the tip. Offer the spoon to your baby gently.

The first feeding is a very exciting and memorable moment, but do not get your hopes up too soon. It is indeed possible that your baby will not be interested in the food. If that happens, do NOT try to force feed them. Just allow the baby to smell the food and try again another time.

Another important thing you should pay attention to is the time. Feed the baby around the same time each day, and make sure it is before noon. This will give you plenty of time during the day to watch for any unwanted food reactions.

INTRODUCING NEW FOODS

New ingredients should be introduced gradually. Feed your baby the same ingredient for three days, then introduce a new one. Feed them with the new food ingredient for three days, and then introduce another one. After they have sampled a couple of ingredients, you can them start mixing and matching, but I do not recommend offering more than two ingredients at once the first month.

A great thing to do is keep a log of your baby's feedings. This way you will know exactly what your baby has sampled and when, as well as allow you to rule out possible allergies. Also, this is a great way of keeping a track of the already consumed foods and ensure a properly balanced diet and nutrient intake.

HOW MUCH IS ENOUGH?

Just like in the beginning when you were worried about feeding your baby enough breastmilk or formula, it is only natural to be a little afraid you will not be able to determine if your baby has had enough solid food.

Know that your baby's appetite varies just like yours does. There isn't a strict amount you should always stick to, so let your baby take the lead. If your baby shows the signs below, they are probably full:

- Looks away when you offer him food
- Leans back in chair

- Turns the head away from the food
- Begins playing with the spoon
- Doesn't open the mouth

However, the approximate amount of food babies should eat per day is:

6 months

Start with a teaspoon or two of pureed food once a day, and increase slowly to one tablespoon of pureed solids or cereals, twice a day.

6 – 8 months

One teaspoon of vegetables increased to two–three tbsp in three feedings, gradually.

One teaspoon of fruits gradually increased to two-three tablespoons in three feedings

Three-nine tablespoons of cereal in two-three meals

Two tablespoons of protein foods

8 – 10 months

¼ - ⅓ cup Dairy

¼ - ½ cup Cereal

¾ - 1 cup Fruit

¾ - 1 cup Vegetables

3 – 4 tbsp Protein Foods

10 – 12 months

Same as the previous category, but the overall food intake should be increased by ¼ – ½ cup a day.

FEEDING TIPS

<u>Offer foods in any order.</u> Some may claim there is a certain pattern. For instance, you should start with cereals, then veggies, then fruits, but if you don't feel like it, you can give your baby foods in any particular order.

<u>Feed your baby cereal only with a spoon.</u> Unless your doctor recommends, always feed the cereal with a spoon only. Adding cereal to the bottle is not suggested not only because your baby can gain too much weight that way, but also because there is the hazard of choking.

<u>Give it time.</u> Just because your baby doesn't like avocados doesn't mean he will never eat an avocado puree. Be persistent and try again in a few days.

<u>Watch out for constipation.</u> When your baby starts eating solids, it is most likely his stool will change. Constipation is usually a temporary condition, but when it happens, tell your pediatrician. Your doctor may advise you to include high-fiber foods or omit certain ingredients altogether.

WHAT ABOUT BREASTFEEDING OR BOTTLE FEEDING?

Keep in mind that breastmilk or formula will still provide the majority of the calories, as well as the nutrients, even after starting with solids. Both breastmilk and formula provide super-digestible nutrients that solid foods cannot replace, and therefore are recommended throughout the first year of baby's life.

Instant Pot for Babies Intro

Making homemade food for babies is far healthier and more nutritious than buying jarred purees. However, simply dumping veggies and boiling them on the stove will not provide adequate nutrition. When it comes to your baby's growth and progress, it is your job to ensure the consumption of all the essential nutrients. And the best way to do it? In the Instant Pot, of course.

The Instant Pot is a revolutionary kitchen appliance that wears the crown among all electric pressure cookers. Its super functionality and convenient cooking process allow you to put healthy, delicious meals on your table quickly and nearly effortlessly.

Besides its amazingly simple usage and the fact that it can help you save time and money by cooking the meals seventy percent quicker than the traditional cooking methods, cooking in the Instant Pot is also much healthier.

If you are a proud Instant Pot owner, you are probably familiar with all that and know that the IP is a real crowd pleaser and especially designed to satisfy the needs of your entire family. But what is even more amazing is that it is also perfect for feeding even the smallest tummy in your family – your baby's.

But why prepare baby's purees in the Instant Pot? Because that way, your baby will consume more nutrients.

You know how all doctors and nutritionists suggest steaming instead of boiling your veggies because during the process of boiling most of their nutrients get lost in the water? Well, the Instant Pot preserves even those nutrients that are lost during the steaming process.

Thanks to its excellent pressure cooking technology, the Instant Pot cooks the food quickly without destroying its natural nutrients. This is especially important for babies since almost every fruit or veggie they should try in the beginning (except banana and avocado) should be cooked.

If that still doesn't sell it, perhaps this will – *the Instant Pot completely destroys all the possible harmful properties found in the food.* Although buying 100%

natural and organic food is a great way to ensure proper nutrient consumption, it is possible for the food to still be contaminated in some way. Because the Instant Pot always cooks at temperatures above the point of boiling water, you can rest assured that all the harmful properties will be destroyed during the cooking process.

This is extremely useful for those of you who live in high altitude places where the air pressure is low, because there the water reaches boiling temperature at a much lower temperature.

Cooking Charts for Baby's Food

Just because choosing to prepare your baby's foods in the Instant Pot ensures nutrient preserving doesn't mean you cannot destroy them. If you let your broccoli cook on HIGH pressure for half an hour, that will surely result in loss of essential vitamins and nutrients. That being said, it is important for you to know exactly how long you should pressure cook each type of fruit to make sure the baby's puree will be rich in all the nutrients that will help your baby's growth and progress.

Here is the cooking charts for purees and cereal divided into six categories: vegetables, fruits, grains, beans, meat, and fish and seafood.

VEGETABLES

Type of Vegetable	Fresh (Cooking Time on "STEAM")	Frozen (Cooking Time on "STEAM")
Artichokes, whole	9 - 11 min	11 – 13 min
Artichoke hearts	4 – 5 min	5 – 6 min
Asparagus Spears	2 min	3 min
Beetroot, halved	13 min	15 min
Beetroot, whole	22 min	25 – 30 min
Broccoli florets	2 min	3 min
Brussel Sprouts	3 min	4 min
Cabbage, shredded	3 min	4 min

Cabbage, wedges	4 - 5 min	5 - 6 min
Carrots, sliced	3 min	4 min
Carrots, chunks or whole	6 - 8 min	7 – 9 min
Cauliflower florets	2 – 3 min	3 – 4 min
Celery chunks	2 – 3 min	3 – 4 min
Collard Greens	4 – 5 min	5 – 6 min
Corn kernels	2 min	3 min
Corn on the cob	3 – 5 min	4 – 6 min
Eggplant chunks	4 min	4 – 5 min
Green Beans	3 min	3 – 4 min
Greens, chopped	2 – 3 min	4 – 7 min
Leeks	2 – 3 min	3 – 4 min
Okra	2 – 3 min	3 – 4 min
Onions, sliced	2 – 3 min	3 – 4 min
Parsnips, chopped	3 – 4 min	4 – 5 min
Peas, green	1 – 2 min	2 – 3 min
Baby Potatoes, whole	8 – 10 min	12 – 14 min
Potatoes, whole	12 – 15 min	15 – 19 min
Pumpkin, chopped	2 – 3 min	4 – 5 min
Rutabaga, chopped	4 – 6 min	6 – 8 min
Spinach	1 – 2 min	3 – 4 min
Squash, sliced	4 – 6 min	6 – 8 min
Sweet Potatoes, whole	12 – 15 min	17 – 19 min
Small Sweet Potatoes, whole	8 – 10 min	12 – 14 min
Sweet Peppers	2 – 3 min	3 – 4 min
Tomatoes, quartered	2 – 3 min	4 – 5 min
Zucchini	1 – 3 min	2 – 4 min

FRUITS

Type of Fruit	Fresh (Cooking Time on "STEAM")	Frozen (Cooking Time on "STEAM")
Apples, sliced	1 – 2 min	2 – 3 min
Apples, whole	3 – 4 min	4 – 6 min
Peaches	2 – 3 min	4 – 5 min
Pears, whole	3 – 4 min	4 – 5 min
Pears, sliced or halved	2 – 3 min	4 – 5 min
Plums	2 – 3 min	4 – 5 min

These are the types of fruits that you should definitely be cooking for the first two months or so. Other fruits like mangos, papaya, pineapples, blueberries, etc. should also be cooked during that period. Generally, two to three minutes should do.

GRAINS

Type of Grain	Cooking Time (on "MANUAL")
Barley, pearl	20 – 22 min
Barley, pot	25 – 30 min
Couscous	3 min
Millet	10 – 12 min
Oats, steel cut	3 – 5 min
Rice, Brown	22 – 25 min
Rice, White	4 – 6 min
Quinoa, quick cooking	1 min

MEAT

Type of Meat	Cooking Time (on "MANUAL")
Beef, meatball	8 – 10 min
Beef, small chunks	15 min per
Beef, large chunks	20 minutes
Boneless Chicken Breast, chopped	6 – 8 min

Chicken, whole	6 – 8 min per lb
Lamb, cubes	12 – 15 min
Pork, loin roast	20 min per lb
Pork, butt roast	15 min per lb
Boneless Turkey Breast, chopped	7 – 9 min

FISH and SEAFOOD

Type of Seafood	Fresh (Cooking Time on "STEAM")	Frozen (Cooking Time on "STEAM")
Fish, whole	4 – 5 min	5 – 7 min
Fish filet	2 – 3 min	3 – 4 min
Lobster	3 – 4 min	4 – 6 min
Shrimp and Prawns	1 – 3 min	2 – 4 min

Sample Food Introduction Schedule

Although you should really start with what you feel is right, and of course, what your pediatrician orders, this next food introduction schedule is the most accepted.

Obviously, this is not set in stone and you do not have to follow it day by day. However, this sample schedule is a great way for you to gain understanding of what your baby puree schedule should look like in the first six months.

Week 1:

Day 1: Sweet Potato Puree

Day 2: Sweet Potato Puree

Day 3: Sweet Potato Puree

Day 4: Avocado Puree

Day 5: Avocado Puree

Day 6: Avocado Puree

Day 7: Carrot Puree

Week 2:

Day 1: Carrot Puree

Day 2: Carrot Puree

Day 3: Pea Puree

Day 4: Pea Puree

Day 5: Pea Puree

Day 6: Squash Puree

Day 7: Squash Puree

Week 3:

Day 1: White Rice Cereal

Day 2: White Rice Cereal

Day 3: White Rice Cereal

Day 4: White Rice Cereal

Day 5: Baby Potato and Pea Puree

Day 6: Applesauce

Day 7: Applesauce

WEEK 4:

Day 1: Applesauce

Day 2: Pumpkin Puree

Day 3: Pumpkin Puree

Day 4: Pumpkin Puree

Day 5: Parsnip and Carrot Puree

Day 6: Parsnip and Carrot Puree

Day 7: Parsnip and Carrot Puree

WEEK 5:

Day 1: Meal 1: Brown Rice Cereal, Meal 2: Banana and Avocado Puree

Day 2: Meal 1: Brown Rice Cereal, Meal 2: Apple and Carrot Puree

Day 3: Meal 1: Brown Rice Cereal, Meal 2: Apple and Pumpkin Puree

Day 4: Meal 1: Peach Puree, Meal 2: Green Pea Rice Cereal

Day 5: Meal 1: Peach Puree, Meal 2: Apple Cereal

Day 6: Meal 1: Peach Puree, Meal 2: Parsnip and Avocado Puree

Day 7: Meal 1: Apple and Banana Puree, Meal 2: Squash and Avocado Puree

WEEK 6:

Day 1: Meal 1: Apple and Banana Puree, Meal 2: Carrot and Parsnip Cereal

Day 2: Meal 1: Apple and Banana Puree, Meal 2: Potato and Pea Puree

Day 3: Meal 1: Bean and Carrot Puree, Meal 2: Banana Cereal

Day 4: Meal 1: Bean and Carrot Puree, Meal 2: Avocado and Sweet Potato Puree

Day 5: Meal 1: Bean and Carrot Puree, Meal 2: Pumpkin Puree

Day 6: Meal 1: Beef and Potato Stew, Meal 2: Brown Rice and Peach

Day 7: Meal 1: Beef and Parsnip Puree, Meal 2: Avocado Rice

Of course, you can mix and match different ingredients, but it is important to offer one new ingredient a day and feed your baby that same ingredient for three days to avoid any complications. Next, you can offer your baby oats for three days, yolks, barley, quinoa, chicken, etc.

Healthy Foods

One of the most important parts of feeding your baby solid food is that the food should be organic and healthy. And when I say healthy, I mean super healthy. These are the most important superfoods your baby should be eating the first weeks after introducing solids:

Avocados. One of the healthiest food on the planet, this green fruit is jam-packed with the healthiest fats and will boost your baby's immune system instantly.

Sweet Potatoes. Rich in phytonutrients, sweet potatoes will boost your baby's intake of vitamins C and E. In fact, your baby's first puree can be made with sweet potatoes.

Butternut Squash. Besides its amazingly sweet taste babies love, butternut squash is also a great source of folate, B-vitamins, vitamin C, fiber, omega 3-fatty acids, and potassium.

Apples. Rich in the best vitamins, some of the most powerful antioxidants, and an amazing source of fiber, apples are more than just a sweet treat. They will boost your baby's health and bring a smile to his face.

Peas. Peas are more than a cheap side. They are packed with anti-oxidants and great at fighting inflammation, and most importantly, they are high in fiber, which will help with your baby's constipation.

Parsnips. Rich in folate, potassium, Vitamin C, and fiber, parsnips are a great addition to the beginning of your baby's solid diet. They are not only great with carrots, but you can also combine them with sweet apples.

Carrots. We are all aware of the health benefits of this orange veggie. Loaded with antioxidants and fiber, an amazing source of beta-carotene and vitamin K, carrots should be one of the first veggies to offer to your baby.

Brown Rice. Although white rice should be the first grain to offer your little one, brown rice is the next grain on the line. Packed with manganese and amazingly beneficial properties for the health of the heart, brown rice is the perfect source of fiber that should be introduced in the first weeks.

Other healthy foods that you should definitely introduce to your baby the first weeks are:

- Peaches
- Pumpkin
- Pears
- Green Beans
- Plums
- Rutabaga

Allergies and Food Delaying

Although the safest approach is to introduce new ingredients gradually, and only one at a time, there are certain types of foods known as allergens because of the high risk for allergic reactions.

For that reason, these ingredients are delayed and introduced later, once your baby is used to eating solids and all sorts of different ingredients.

Just to make something clear. No, this isn't a guarantee that your baby will not be allergic to these particular food types. But isn't it better to deal with the unwanted consequences once your baby is strong enough to fight them? That is why the most common allergens shouldn't be offered to your little one the first year of his life, not because that will magically diminish their effect.

Here is the ultimate food chart and when these types of foods should be offered to your baby:

The First Bites (Six Months)

Veggies: Sweet potatoes, potatoes, peas, carrots, parsnips, pumpkin, rutabaga, squash.

Fruits: Bananas, avocados, peaches, plums, apples, pears, nectarines.

Grains: White rice, brown rice.

Dairy: None

Eggs: None

Meat: None

Fish: None

6 – 8 Months

Veggies: Same as before plus: zucchini, broccoli, cauliflower, eggplant, beans, beets, lentils, onions, garlic, turnips, bell peppers, asparagus, green beans, spinach, kale, mushrooms, soy (including tofu).

<u>Fruits:</u> Same as before plus: blueberries, papaya, pineapples, melon, grapes, apricots, kiwi.

<u>Grains:</u> Same as before plus: oats, barley, quinoa, rye, wheat, pasta.

<u>Dairy:</u> Yogurt, sour cream, cheese.

<u>Eggs:</u> Only the yolk.

<u>Meat:</u> Chicken, beef, turkey, lamb.

<u>Fish:</u> None

<u>Other:</u> Herbs and spices (such as basil, rosemary, thyme, parsley, cumin, turmeric powder, garlic powder, paprika, etc.), flax seeds, sesame seeds.

10 Months

Everything is the same except that this month you can also introduce tomatoes and okra

12 Months

Around baby's birthday, you can introduce the most harmful allergens:

- Cow's milk
- Egg whites
- Citrus fruits
- Berries (except blueberries, which can be introduced earlier)
- Peanuts and peanut butter
- Honey
- Shellfish

RECOGNIZING ALLERGY REACTIONS

No matter how careful you are, if your baby is prone to allergies, there is no way to avoid that. The only way you can do for your baby is to monitor his condition closely, watch for allergic reactions, and seek medical help immediately.

Usually, the signs of an allergy are visible minutes or hours after the meal:

- − Vomiting
- − Hives
- − Diarrhea

If your baby has facial swelling, difficulty breathing, or if you notice wheezing, contact 911 immediately, as those are signs of a life-threatening allergic reaction called *anaphylaxis.*

6 Months

STAGE 1: First Bites

This month you should offer your baby runny, thin purees made with the allowed ingredients only. Start gradually by introducing single-ingredient purees and by offering a teaspoon or two, and increase to one or two tablespoons.

Sweet Potato Puree

Preparation time: 5 minutes

Cooking time: 5 minutes

Servings: 4

Ingredients:

1 sweet potato, cut into chunks

1 cup water

Instructions:

Pour the water into your Instant Pot and place the sweet potato chunks inside. Put the lid on and turn it clockwise to close it. You will know it is sealed once you hear the chime. Press "MANUAL" and set the cooking time to 5 minutes by pressing the "+" and "-" buttons.

When you hear the beeping sound, press "KEEP WARM/CANCEL" to turn the IP off. Release the pressure quickly by moving the pressure release handle from "Sealing" to "Venting". Make sure to keep your hands away from the steam to avoid burning.

Transfer the potato chunks to a bowl and add about ⅓ cup of the cooking liquid, but reserve the rest. Blend the mixture with a hand blender until smooth. If the consistency is not thin enough for your baby, add more of the cooking liquid.

Place the leftovers in an airtight container and refrigerate for up to three days or divide between an ice cube tray or a baby food tray and freeze for up to three months.

Pea Puree

Preparation time: 5 minutes
Cooking time: 3 ½ minutes
Servings: 3-4

Ingredients:

1 cup Green Peas

1 ½ cups water

Instructions:

Pour the water into your Instant Pot. Place the green peas inside the steamer basket. Lower the basket into the water and close the lid by turning it clockwise. You should hear the chime. Press "MANUAL" and set the cooking time to 3 ½ minutes by pressing the "+" and "-" buttons.

When you hear the beeping sound, press "KEEP WARM/CANCEL" and turn it off. Move the pressure release handle from "Sealing" to "Venting" and release the pressure quickly.

Remove the steamer basket and transfer the cooked peas to a bowl. Add about ¼ - ⅓ cup of the cooking liquid to the bowl. Blend with a hand blender until smooth. If you want a thinner consistency, add more of the cooking liquid.

Place the leftovers in an airtight container and refrigerate for up to three days. If you want to freeze them, divide between an ice cube tray or a baby food tray and place in the freezer. They should be safe to eat for up to three months.

Carrot Puree

Preparation time: 5 minutes
Cooking time: 8 minutes
Servings: 5

Ingredients:

3 Carrots, peeled and cut into thirds

1 ½ cups water

¼ cup Breastmilk or Formula

Instructions:

Pour the water into your Instant Pot. Place the carrots inside the steamer basket and lower it into the pot. Turn the lid clockwise to close it. The chiming sound will signal the proper sealing. Press "STEAM" and set the cooking time to 8 minutes by pressing the "+" and "-" buttons.

When the IP beeps and screen reads 0:00, press "CANCEL". Do a quick pressure release by turning the pressure release handle to "Venting". Be careful not to burn yourself.

Remove the steamer basket and transfer the carrot chunks to a bowl, but reserve the cooking liquid. Add the milk or formula and blend with a hand blender until smooth. You will probably need to add a few tablespoons of the water for a thinner consistency.

The leftovers can be stored in the fridge (in an airtight container) for three days, or frozen for up to two weeks in the freezer inside the refrigerator or three to six months in a self-contained freezer.

Pureed Squash

Preparation time: 5 minutes
Cooking time: 6 minutes
Servings: 3

Ingredients:

1 cup Butternut Squash Slices, peeled

1 cup water

Instructions:

Pour the water into your Instant Pot and lower the steamer basket. Drop the squash slices into the basket and put the lid on. Turn clockwise to seal. Set the Instant Pot to "STEAM" and set the cooking time to 6 minutes.

When you hear the beeping sound, press "CANCEL" to turn off the IP. Move the pressure release handle from "Sealing" to "Venting" and release the pressure quickly.

Transfer the squash slices from the steamer basket to a bowl and reserve the water in the pot. Blend with a hand blender while pouring some of the cooking liquid until the consistency is thin to your liking.

Store the leftovers in the fridge for three days or in the freezer for up to three months.

Applesauce

Preparation time: 10 minutes
Cooking time: 3 minutes
Servings: 6-8

Ingredients:

4 Gala Apples, quartered and cored

1 ½ cup Water

Instructions:

Pour the water into your Instant Pot and lower the steamer basket. Place the apple quarters into the basket and put the lid on. Turn it clockwise to seal. After the chiming sound, press "STEAM". Set the cooking time to 3 minutes with the help of the "+" and "-" buttons.

Press "CANCEL" to turn off the IP after the timer goes off. Move the pressure release handle from "Sealing" to "Venting" for a quick pressure release.

Drain the apple slices (but reserve the cooking liquid) and place in a bowl. Let cook until safe to handle. Peel the apples and pour 6-8 tablespoons of the cooking liquid to the bowl. Blend with a hand blender until smooth. Add more water if the puree is not thin enough for your baby.

Store the leftovers in the fridge for three days or in the freezer for up to three months.

White Rice Cereal

Preparation time: 5 minutes
Cooking time: 5 minutes
Servings: 4 (about 1 cup of Rice Cereal)

Ingredients:

¼ cup Rice

⅔ cup Water

¼ cup Breastmilk or Formula

Instructions:

Place the rice in a food processor and pulse until finely ground.

Combine the ground rice and water in the Instant Pot. Turn the lid clockwise to seal. Set the Instant Pot to "MANUAL" and cook on HIGH pressure for 5 minutes.

When you hear the beeping sound, press "CANCEL" to turn off the IP. Let the pressure drop naturally by allowing the float valve to go down on its own.

Open the lid and stir in the breastmilk. If the consistency is not thin enough for your baby, stir in more milk.

Store the leftovers in the fridge for three days or in the freezer inside your fridge for up to two weeks. The cereal can be stored in a self-contained freezer for up to three-six months.

Brown Rice Cereal

Preparation time: 5 minutes
Cooking time: 25 minutes
Servings: 4 (about 1 cup of Rice Cereal)

Ingredients:

¼ cup Brown Rice

⅔ cup Water

¼ cup Breastmilk or Formula

Instructions:

Place the rice in a food processor and pulse until finely ground.

Combine the ground rice and water in the Instant Pot. Turn the lid clockwise to seal. Set the Instant Pot to "MANUAL" and cook on HIGH pressure for 25 minutes.

Press "CANCEL" after the timer goes off and turn off the IP. Allow a natural pressure release, by letting the float valve come to a down position on its own. Open the lid and stir in the breastmilk. You may need to add more milk if your baby cannot handle the consistency.

Store the leftovers in the fridge for three days or in the freezer inside your fridge for up to two weeks. The cereal can be stored in a self-contained freezer for up to three-six months.

Pumpkin Puree

Preparation time: 5 minutes
Cooking time: 3 ½ minutes
Servings: 4

Ingredients:

1 cup small cubes of Pumpkin

1 cup Water

Instructions:

Combine the pumpkin cubes and water in the Instant Pot. Put the lid on and turn it clockwise to seal. Press "MANUAL". Set the IP to HIGH pressure and the cooking time to 3 ½ minutes.

When you hear the beeping sound, press "KEEP WARM/CANCEL" to turn off. Do a quick pressure release by moving the handle to "Venting". Open the lid. Drain the pumpkin and transfer to a bowl, but reserve the cooking liquid. Add some of the liquid to the bowl. This depends on the consistency your baby can handle, but ¼ to ⅓ cup should be enough. Blend the mixture until smooth.

Store in airtight container in the fridge for three days or freeze in an ice cube tray for up to three months.

Parsnip and Carrot Puree

Preparation time: 5 minutes
Cooking time: 5 minutes
Servings: 4

Ingredients:

½ cup sliced Carrots

½ cup small Parsnip chunks

1 cup Water

Instructions:

Pour the water into the Instant Pot. Combine the carrots and parsnip inside the steamer basket. Lower it into the pot. Close and seal the lid by turning it clockwise. Set the Instant Pot to "STEAM" and the cooking time to 4 minutes.

When the timer goes off and the screen reads 0:00, press "KEEP WARM/ CANCEL" to turn off. Do a quick pressure release by moving the pressure release handle from "Sealing" to "Venting". Open the lid. Drain the veggies and transfer to a bowl, but reserve the cooking liquid. Blend the veggies with a hand blender along with ¼ cup of the liquid. Add more liquid for thinner consistency.

Store in airtight container in the fridge for three days or freeze in an ice cube tray for up to three months.

Baby Potato and Pea Puree

Preparation time: 10 minutes
Cooking time: 11 minutes
Servings: 6

Ingredients:

6 Baby Potatoes

½ cup Green Peas

1 ½ cups Water

Instructions:

Pour the water into the IP. Wash the baby potatoes well and place them inside the steamer basket. Close the lid of the pot by turning it clockwise. You will know it's sealed after the chiming sound. Press "STEAM" and set the cooking time to 7 minutes.

When you hear the beeping sound, press "KEEP WARM/CANCEL" to turn off. Do a quick pressure release by moving the handle to "Venting". Open the lid. Add the peas to the basket and close the lid again. Select "STEAM" again and cook for 3 ½ minutes.

When the timer goes off, press "CANCEL". Again, do a quick pressure release. Open the lid and drain the veggies, but reserve the water in the pot. Let the potatoes cool a bit until safe to handle. Peel and place in a bowl along with the peas and ⅓ cup of the cooking water. Blend with a and blend until smooth. Add more water if you are looking for a thinner consistency.

Store in airtight container in the fridge for three days or freeze in an ice cube tray for up to three months.

Peach Puree

Preparation time: 5 minutes
Cooking time: 5 minutes
Servings: 2

Ingredients:

1 Peach, peeled and halved

1 cup Water

Instructions:

Pour the water into the Instant Pot and lower the rack. Place the peaches in an ovenproof bowl and place on the rack. Put the lid on and turn it clockwise to seal. Press "STEAM". With the help of the "+" and "-" buttons, set the cooking time to 3 minutes.

After the beeping sound, press "KEEP WARM/CANCEL" to turn the IP off. Do a quick pressure release by moving the pressure handle to "Venting". Be careful not to keep your hands near the steam. Open the lid. Add a few tablespoons of the cooking liquid to the bowl with peaches and blend with a hand blender. You should aim for a thin consistency the baby can handle.

Store in airtight container in the fridge for three days or freeze in an ice cube tray for up to three months.

Apple and Banana Puree

Preparation time: 8 minutes

Cooking time: 3 minutes

Servings: 3

Ingredients:

1 cup cubed of peeled Apple

1 small Banana, cut into chunks

1 cup Water

Instructions:

Place the apple cubes in a baking dish or heatproof container. Pour the water into the IP and lower the rack. Place the dish or bowl on the rack and put the lid on. Seal by turning it clockwise. You should hear a chime. Press "STEAM" and cook for 2-3 minutes.

When you hear the beeping sound, press "KEEP WARM/CANCEL" to turn off. Move the pressure release handle to "Venting" to let the pressure out all at once. Open the lid.

Add the banana chunks to the bowl with apples and add about ¼ cup of the cooking water. Blend with a hand blender until smooth. If not thin enough, blend in more water.

Store in an airtight container in the fridge for three days or freeze in an ice cube tray or a baby food tray for up to three months.

Avocado and Sweet Potato Puree

Preparation time: 5 minutes
Cooking time: 5 minutes
Servings: 4

Ingredients:

½ Sweet Potato, peeled and cut into chunks

½ Avocado, flesh scooped out

1 cup Water

Instructions:

Combine the potato and water in the Instant Pot. Put the lid on and turn it clockwise to seal. You should hear a chime. Press "STEAM". Set the cooking time to 5 minutes.

When the timer goes off, press "KEEP WARM/CANCEL" to turn the Instant Pot off. Do a quick pressure release by moving the handle to "Venting". Open the lid. Drain the sweet potato cubes and transfer to a bowl, but reserve the cooking liquid. Add the avocado and some of the cooking liquid (about ¼ cup) to the bowl. Blend with a hand blender. If looking for a thinner consistency, add more water.

Store in airtight container in the fridge for three days or freeze in an ice cube tray for up to three months.

Peachy Rice Cereal

Preparation time: 5 minutes
Cooking time: 8 minutes
Servings: 4

Ingredients:

¼ cup Rice

½ Peach, chopped

⅔ cup Water

¼ cup Breastmilk or Formula

Instructions:

Place the rice in a food processor and pulse until ground. Transfer to the Instant Pot.

Pour the water into the IP and stir to combine. Put the lid on and turn it clockwise to seal. Press "MANUAL". Set the IP to HIGH pressure and the cooking time to 3 minutes.

When you hear the beeping sound, press "KEEP WARM/CANCEL" to turn off. Do a quick pressure release by moving the handle to "Venting". Stir in the chopped peach and put the lid on. Seal the lid again and set the cooking time to 2 ½ minutes on HIGH.

Do a quick pressure release after the timer goes off. Stir the milk or formula into the cereal.

Store in airtight container in the fridge for three days or freeze in an ice cube tray for up to two weeks. Stored in a self-contained freezer the cereal can last for up to three-six months.

Pear Puree

Preparation time: 5 minutes
Cooking time: 5 minutes
Servings: 6

Ingredients:

3 Pears, peeled, cored, and halved

1 cup Water

Instructions:

Pour the water into the Instant Pot. Place the pears inside the steamer basket and lower the basket into the IP. Put the lid on and seal it by turning it clockwise. Press "STEAM". Set the cooking time to 3 minutes.

When the screen reads 0:00, press "KEEP WARM/CANCEL" to turn off. Do a quick pressure release by moving the handle to "Venting". Open the lid carefully and transfer the pears to a bowl. Pour some of the cooking liquid (about ¼ - ⅓ cup) into the bowl. Blend with a hand blender until really smooth.

Store in airtight container in the fridge for three days or freeze in an ice cube tray for up to three months.

Brown Rice Cereal with Plums

Preparation time: 5 minutes
Cooking time: 25 minutes
Servings: 4

Ingredients:

¼ cup Brown Rice

⅔ cup Wate

1 Plum, halved

¼ cup Breastmilk or Formula

Instructions:

Place the rice in a food processor and pulse until ground. Transfer to the Instant Pot.Stir the water into the IP and put the lid on. Turn clockwise until you hear the chime. Press "MANUAL". Set the IP to HIGH pressure and the cooking time to 22 minutes.

When you hear the beeping sound, press "KEEP WARM/CANCEL" to turn off. Do a quick pressure release by moving the handle to "Venting". Open the lid and place the plum inside. Close the lid again and cook for another 5 minutes on HIGH.

Allow for the pressure valve to drop on its own. Open the lid and pour the milk over. Blend with a hand blender until smooth.

Store in airtight container in the fridge for three days or freeze for up to two weeks. A self-contained freezer can keep the cereal safe for up to three-six months.

Potato and Rice Puree

Preparation time: 5 minutes
Cooking time: 5 minutes
Servings: 4

Ingredients:

1 cup chopped peeled Potatoes

3 tbsp Rice

1 ¼ cup Water

Instructions:

Place the rice in a food processor and pulse until ground. Transfer to the Instant Pot. Add the rest of the ingredients and stir to combine. Put the lid on and turn it clockwise to seal. Press "MANUAL". Set the IP to HIGH pressure and the cooking time to 5 minutes.

Press "KEEP WARM/CANCEL" after the timer goes off. Release the pressure naturally by letting the valve come down on its own. Open the lid. Blend the mixture inside the pot with a hand blender until smooth. If needed, add some more baby water to the pot.

Store in airtight container in the fridge for three days or freeze in an ice cube tray for up to three months.

Apple Cereal

Preparation time: 5 minutes
Cooking time: 5 minutes
Servings: 4

Ingredients:

¼ cup White Rice

1 Apple, peeled, cored, and halved

⅔ cup Water

Instructions:

Place the rice in a food processor and pulse until ground. Transfer to the Instant Pot.

Add the rest of the ingredients and stir to combine. Put the lid on and turn it clockwise to seal. Press "MANUAL". Set the IP to HIGH pressure and the cooking time to 5 minutes.

Press "KEEP WARM/CANCEL" after the timer goes off. Allow a natural pressure release until the float valve drops on its own. Open the lid. Blend the mixture inside the pot with a hand blender until smooth. If needed, add more water to the pot.

Store in airtight container in the fridge for three days or freeze in an ice cube tray for up to three months.

Carrot and Apple Puree

Preparation time: 5 minutes
Cooking time: 5 minutes
Servings: 4

Ingredients:

½ cup sliced Carrots

2 Gala Apples, peeled, cored, and halved

3 tbsp Rice

1 ¼ cup Water

Instructions:

Pour the water into the Instant Pot and lower the steamer basket. Dump the carrots and apples into the basket and put the lid on. Close and seal by turning it clockwise until you hear the chime. Press "STEAM" and set the cooking time for 5 minutes.

Press "KEEP WARM/CANCEL" after the beeping sound. Do a quick pressure release by turning the pressure release handle to "Venting".

Transfer the mixture to a bowl and add a few tablespoons of the cooking liquid. Blend with a hand blender until smooth.

Store in airtight container in the fridge for three days or freeze in an ice cube tray for up to three months.

Green Pea Rice Cereal

Preparation time: 5 minutes
Cooking time: 5 minutes
Servings: 6

Ingredients:

½ cup Green Peas

¼ cup White Rice

1 cup Water

Instructions:

Place the rice in a food processor and pulse until ground. Transfer to the Instant Pot.

Add the rest of the ingredients and stir to combine. Put the lid on and turn it clockwise to seal. Select "MANUAL" and cook for 5 minutes on HIGH pressure.

Press "KEEP WARM/CANCEL" after you hear the beeping sound. Let the pressure come down naturally by letting the valve come down on its own. Open the lid. Blend the mixture inside the pot with a hand blender until smooth. If the consistency is not thin, blend in water.

Store in airtight container in the fridge for three days or freeze in an ice cube tray for up to three months.

6 – 8 Months

STAGE 2: Creamy Combos

Your baby is now ready to try different flavors. You can introduce beans, meat, yolks, more grains, and spice things up with herbs, spices, and some aromatics like garlic and onion. The purees shouldn't be that thin, but much thicker and with a rich and creamy texture.

Peach Oatmeal

Preparation time: 5 minutes
Cooking time: 5 minutes
Servings: 2

Ingredients:

¼ cup Steel-Cut Oats

1 Peach, peeled and halved

¾ cup Water

Instructions:

Place the oats in a food processor and pulse until ground. Transfer to the Instant Pot.

Add the rest of the ingredients and stir to combine. Put the lid on and turn it clockwise to seal. Press "MANUAL". Set the cooking time to 5 minutes and cook on HIGH pressure.

Press "KEEP WARM/CANCEL" after the timer goes off. Let the float valve come down on its own naturally. Open the lid. Blend the mixture inside the pot with a hand blender until smooth. If a thinner consistency is needed, add some formula or breastmilk to it.

Store in airtight container in the fridge for three days or freeze in an ice cube tray for up to three months. If using formula or breastmilk, the oatmeal can be frozen for up to two weeks.

Pear and Avocado Puree with Yogurt

Preparation time: 5 minutes

Cooking time: 3 minutes

Servings: 2-3

Ingredients:

1 Avocado, flesh scooped out

1 Pear, peeled, cored, and halved

1 cup Water

⅓ cup Greek Yogurt

Instructions:

Pour the water into the Instant Pot. Place the pear halves inside the steamer basket and lower the basket into the IP. Close the lid by turning it clockwise. Press "STEAM" and cook for 3 minutes.

Press "KEEP WARM/CANCEL" after the timer goes off. Move the pressure handle to "Venting" immediately to release the pressure quickly. Open the lid and transfer the pear to a bowl. Add the avocado and yogurt to the bowl and blend with a hand blender until smooth. Store in airtight container in the fridge for three days or freeze in an ice cube tray for up to one to two months.

Green Bean and Carrot Puree

Preparation time: 5 minutes

Cooking time: 3 minutes

Servings: 3

Ingredients:

1 cup Green Beans

1 cup Water

1 Carrot, sliced

3 tbsp Greek Yogurt

Instructions:

Pour the water into the Instant Pot. Combine the carrot slices and green beans inside the steamer basket and lower the basket into the IP. Close the lid by turning it clockwise. Press "STEAM" and cook for 3 minutes.

When you hear the beeping sound, press "KEEP WARM/CANCEL". Move the pressure handle to "Venting" immediately, to release the pressure quickly. Open the lid and transfer the veggies to a bowl. Add the yogurt and blend until smooth.

Store in airtight container in the fridge for three days or freeze in an ice cube tray for up to one to two months.

Parsnip, Green Bean, and Sour Cream Puree

Preparation time: 5 minutes
Cooking time: 3 minutes
Servings: 4

Ingredients:

1 Parsnip, peeled and sliced thinly

¾ cup Green Beans

1 ½ cup Water

2-3 tbsp Sour Cream

Instructions:

Pour the water into the Instant Pot and lower the steamer basket. Dump the vegies into the basket and put the lid on. Close the lid by turning it clockwise. Press "STEAM" and cook for 3 minutes.

Press "KEEP WARM/CANCEL" after the timer goes off. Move the pressure handle to "Venting" and release the pressure quickly. Open the lid and transfer the veggies a bowl. Add the sour cream to the bowl and blend until smooth.

Store in airtight container in the fridge for three days. Freezing is not recommended.

Potato and Egg Yolk Puree

Preparation time: 10 minutes
Cooking time: 8 minutes
Servings: 1-2

Ingredients:

1 Potato, cut in half

1 Egg

1 cup Water

A dollop of Sour Cream

Instructions:

Pour the water into the Instant Pot. Pace the egg and potato inside the steamer basket and lower it. Close the lid by turning it clockwise. Select "MANUAL" and cook for 8 minutes on HIGH pressure.

Press "KEEP WARM/CANCEL" after the timer goes off. Move the pressure handle to "Venting" and release the pressure quickly. Open the lid and remove the egg and potato from the IP. Allow to cool until safe to handle.

Peel the egg and remove the egg yolk. Place it in a bowl. Peel the potato and add to the bowl along with the sour cream. Blend until smooth. Store in airtight container in the fridge for three days. Freezing is not recommended.

Beef and Potato Stew Puree

Preparation time: 5 minutes
Cooking time: 12 minutes
Servings: 4

Ingredients:

2 Whole Potatoes, peeled

½ cup small Beef Cubes

1 ½ cup Water

Instructions:

Place all the ingredients in the Instant Pot. Stir to combine and put the lid on. Seal it by turning it clockwise. When you hear the chime, press "MANUAL". Set the cooking tie to 12 minutes.

Press "KEEP WARM/CANCEL" after the timer goes off. Move the pressure handle to "Venting" and release the pressure quickly. Open the lid and transfer the beef and potatoes to a bowl, but reserve the cooking liquid. Blend the mixture while pouring some of the cooking liquid into it to reach desired consistency. Store in airtight container in the fridge for three days or freeze in an ice cube tray for up to three months.

Bean and Carrot Puree

Preparation time: 5 minutes
Cooking time: 10 minutes
Servings: 4

Ingredients:

1 cup Kidney Beans, soaked overnight, rinsed, and drained

2 Carrots, peeled

1 ½ cup Water

1 tbsp Butter

Pinch of Thyme

Instructions:

Combine the beans, carrots, water, and thyme in the Instant Pot. Close the lid by turning it clockwise. Press "MANUAL" and cook for 10 minutes on HIGH.

Press "CANCEL" after the beep. Move the pressure handle to "Venting" and release the pressure quickly. Open the lid and transfer the beans and carrots to a bowl, but reserve the cooking liquid. Add the butter and some of the cooking liquid (as needed to reach the desired consistency) and blend until smooth.

Store in airtight container in the fridge for three days or freeze for up to three months.

Creamy Veggie Soup

Preparation time: 5 minutes

Cooking time: 5 minutes

Servings: 4

Ingredients:

1 Carrot, chopped

1 Potato, peeled and cut into chunks

½ Parsnip, chopped

⅓ cup chopped Leeks

⅔ cup Water

1 tbsp Butter

1 tsp chopped Basil

A dollop of Sour Cream

Instructions:

Turn on the Instant Pot and set it to SAUTE. Place the butter inside and cook until it is melted. Add the leeks and cook them for about 3 minutes. After they are softened, add the remaining veggies to the pot. Pour the water over and stir in the basil. Put the lid on, then turn it clockwise to seal. After the chiming sound, press "MANUAL" and cook for 5 minutes on HIGH.

Press "CANCEL" after the beep. Move the pressure handle to "Venting" and release the pressure quickly. Open the lid and add the sour cream. Blend the mixture inside the IP with a hand blender, until smooth.

Store in airtight container in the fridge for three days. Freezing is not recommended.

Chicken and Rice Stew

Preparation time: 5 minutes

Cooking time: 8 minutes

Servings: 4

Ingredients:

1 tbsp Olive Oil

1 tbsp chopped Red Onion (or leek if you haven't introduced onion yet)

½ cup small Chicken Cubes

1 Carrot, sliced

¼ cup White Rice

1 cup Water

Pinch of Rosemary

Instructions:

Place the rice in a food processor and pulse until ground.

Set the Instant Pot on "SAUTE". Add the olive oil in it and cook until it is well heated. Add the onions and cook for 2-3 minutes. Then, add the chicken and cook until it is no longer pink. Stir in the carrot, rice, rosemary, and water. Close and seal the lid by turning clockwise. Press "MANUAL" and cook for 8 minutes on HIGH.

Press "CANCEL" after the beep. Move the pressure handle to "Venting" and release the pressure quickly. Blend briefly to mash everything well.

Store in airtight container in the fridge for three days or freeze for up to three months.

Sweet Potato and Spinach Puree with Sour Cream

Preparation time: 5 minutes

Cooking time: 10 minutes

Servings: 2

Ingredients:

1 Sweet Potato, peeled and cut into chunks

½ cup Baby Spinach

A dollop of Sour Cream

1 cup of Water

Instructions:

Pour the water into the IP and place the sweet potato cubes in the steamer basket. Lower the basket and put the lid on. Turn clockwise to seal and set the IP to "STEAM". Cook for 4 minutes.

Press "CANCEL" after the beep. Move the pressure handle to "Venting" and release the pressure quickly. Open the lid and add the spinach to the basket. Close again and set the cooking time for 1 minute. Turn the handle to "Venting" again and transfer the potatoes and spinach to a bowl. Add the sour cream and some of the water if needed. Blend until smooth.

Store in airtight container in the fridge for three days. Freezing is not recommended.

Cheesy Potato and Leek Soup

Preparation time: 5 minutes

Cooking time: 4 minutes

Servings: 4

Ingredients:

1 tbsp Butter

⅓ cup sliced Leek

2 Large Potatoes, diced

⅔ cup low-sodium Chicken Broth or Water

¼ cup shredded Mozzarella Cheese

Pinch of Turmeric Powder

Instructions:

Melt the butter in your Instant Pot on "SAUTE". Add the leek and cook for about 3 minutes until it becomes softened. Then, add the potatoes and turmeric, and pour the broth over. Close and seal the lid. When you hear the chime, press "MANUAL". Set the cooking time for 4 minutes.

Press "CANCEL" after the screen reads 0:00. Move the pressure handle to "Venting" and release the pressure quickly. Open the lid and stir in the mozzarella cheese. Blend the soup until smooth.

Store in airtight container in the fridge for three days or freeze for up to three months.

Vanilla Blueberry Oatmeal

Preparation time: 5 minutes

Cooking time: 10 minutes

Servings: 4

Ingredients:

¼ cup Steel-Cut Oats

¾ cup Water

A drop of Vanilla Extract

3 tbsp Blueberries

Instructions:

Place the oats in your food processor and pulse until ground.

Combine all the ingredients in the Instant Pot. Close the lid by turning it clockwise. When you hear the chime, select "MANUAL" and cook for 5 minutes on HIGH.

Press "CANCEL" after the beep. Move the pressure release handle from "Sealing" to "Venting" and release the pressure quickly. Open the lid and mash with a fork well or just give it a pulse with a hand blender.

Store in airtight container in the fridge for three days or freeze for up to three months.

Chicken and Broccoli Soup with Cheese

Preparation time: 5 minutes
Cooking time: 10 minutes
Servings: 4

Ingredients:

½ cup Broccoli Florets

½ cup diced Chicken Breasts, skinless and boneless

1 Carrot, sliced

1 Potato, peeled and diced

1 cup Water

⅓ cup shredded Cheese

1 tbsp Sour Cream

1 tbsp Butter

1 tbsp chopped Onion or Leek

Instructions:

Set the Instant Pot to "SAUTE" and add the butter. When melted, add the onions and cook until soft, about 3 minutes. Add the chicken and cook until it is no longer pink. Stir in the carrots, potatoes, broccoli, and water. Close the lid by turning it clockwise. Press "MANUAL" and cook for 10 minutes on HIGH.

Press "CANCEL" after the beeping sound. Move the pressure handle to "Venting" to release the pressure quickly. Open the lid and stir in the cheese and sour cream. Blend the soup until smooth.

Store in airtight container in the fridge for three days. Freezing is not recommended.

Potato and Beetroot Swirl

Preparation time: 5 minutes
Cooking time: 10 minutes
Servings: 2

Ingredients:

1 Whole Potato, peeled

½ Beetroot, halved

1 tbsp Yogurt

1 cup Water

Instructions:

Place the beetroot and potato in the steamer basket. Pour the water into the Instant Pot and lower the basket. Put the lid on and seal by turning it clockwise. Press "STEAM" and set the cooking time for 10 minutes on HIGH.

Press "CANCEL" after the beep. Move the pressure release handle to "Venting" for a quick pressure quickly. Open the lid and transfer the veggies to a bowl along with a few tablespoons of the cooking water. Add the yogurt and blend with a hand blender until smooth.

Store in airtight container in the fridge for three days or freeze for up to one to two months.

Beef and Mushroom Stew

Preparation time: 5 minutes
Cooking time: 10 minutes
Servings: 2

Ingredients:

1 Potato, cut into chunks

½ cup diced Beef

1 Carrot, sliced

3 tbsp chopped Green Beans

⅓ cup Mushroom Slices

1 tbsp Olive Oil

1 tbsp chopped Onion

1 cup Water

Instructions:

Set the Instant Pot to "SAUTE" and add the olive oil. When hot, add the onions and cook for 2 minutes. Then, add the mushrooms and cook until they become darkened, about 2 minutes. Add the beef and cook it until it becomes dark. Stir in the remaining ingredients and put the lid on. Seal the pot by turning the lid clockwise. Press "MANUAL" and set the cooking time for 10 minutes. Cook on HIGH pressure.

Press "CANCEL" after the timer goes off. Allow a natural pressure release. When the float valve is down, open the lid. Grab a hand blender and blend the stew inside the pot until you reach the consistency your baby can handle.

Store in airtight container in the fridge for three days or freeze for up to three months.

Mushroom and Pea Quinoa

Preparation time: 5 minutes

Cooking time: 10 minutes

Servings: 3

Ingredients:

¼ cup Quinoa

⅔ cup Water

¼ cup sliced Mushrooms

¼ cup Peas

Pinch of Garlic Powder

Instructions:

Place the quinoa in a food processor and pulse until ground. Transfer to the IP. Stir in the remaining ingredients and close the lid. Seal it well by turning it clockwise. After the chime, select "MANUAL" and set the cooking time for 13 minutes. Cook on LOW pressure.

When the timer goes off, press "KEEP WARM / CANCEL". Let the valve drop on its own for a natural pressure release. Open the lid and give the mixture several pulses with a hand blender until smooth. If needed, add some extra water for thinner consistency.

Store in airtight container in the fridge for three days or freeze for up to three months.

Cauliflower and Asparagus Soup

Preparation time: 5 minutes
Cooking time: 4 minutes
Servings: 2

Ingredients:

½ cup Cauliflower Florets
4 Asparagus Spears
½ Carrot, sliced
¼ cup finely diced Parsnip
2 tbsp shredded Mozzarella Cheese
⅔ cup Water

Instructions:

Combine the cauliflower, carrot, asparagus, and parsnip in your Instant Pot. Put the lid on and seal by turning it clockwise. When you hear the chime, hit "MANUAL". Cook the soup for 4 minutes on HIGH.

After the beeping sound, turn the IP off by pressing "CANCEL". Allow the float valve to go down on its own for a natural pressure release. Open the lid and stir in the cheese. Blend the soup with a hand blender inside the pot until creamy and smooth.

Store in airtight container in the fridge for three days or freeze in an ice cube tray for up to three months.

Cinnamon Banana and Yogurt Barley

Preparation time: 5 minutes
Cooking time: 30 minutes
Servings: 2

Ingredients:

¼ cup Pot Barley

⅔ cup Water

Pinch of Cinnamon

½ Banana

3 tbsp Yogurt

Instructions:

Place the barley in a food processor and pulse until smooth. Transfer to the IP.

Pour the water into the Instant Pot and put the lid on. Turn the lid clockwise. After the chime, press "MANUAL". Cook the barley for 25-30 minutes on HIGH.

Press "CANCEL" after the beep. Allow a natural pressure release, which means wait for the float valve to drop on its own. Open the lid and transfer the cooked barley to a bowl. Add the cinnamon, banana, and yogurt, and blend with a hand blender until smooth.

Store in airtight container in the fridge for three days or freeze for up to one to two months.

Cauliflower, Zucchini, and Egg Yolk

Preparation time: 5 minutes
Cooking time: 5 minutes
Servings: 2

Ingredients:

1 Hardboiled Egg Yolk

½ cup Cauliflower Florets

½ cup chopped Zucchini

1 cup Water

2 tbsp Ricotta Cheese

Instructions:

Place the zucchini and cauliflower in the steamer basket. Pour the water into the IP and lower the basket.

Put the lid on, close, and seal. When you hear the chime, Press "STEAM" and set the cooking time for 3 minutes.

Press "CANCEL" after the beep. Move the pressure release handle to "Venting" for a quick pressure quickly.

Open the lid and transfer the veggies to a bowl. Add the ricotta and blend the mixture with a hand blender until you reach the consistency your baby can handle.

Store in airtight container in the fridge for three days or freeze for up to three months.

Cheesy Polenta

Preparation time: 5 minutes
Cooking time: 30 minutes
Servings: 2

Ingredients:

½ cup Polenta

2 cups Boiling Water

Pinch of Garlic Powder

¼ cup shredded Monterrey Jack Cheese

Instructions:

Combine the polenta, garlic powder, and water in the Instant Pot. Put the lid on and seal it by turning clockwise. Select the "PORRIDGE" cooking mode, and with the help of the "ADJUST" button, select the "MORE" option to increase the cooking time by 10 minutes. This may seem long, but trust me, your baby polenta needs it.

Press "CANCEL" after the beep. Move the pressure release handle to "Venting" for a quick pressure quickly. Open the lid and stir in the cheese.

Store in airtight container in the fridge for three days or freeze for up to one to two months.

9 – 12 Months

STAGE 3: Chunky Combinations and Finger Foods

It is time for your baby to use his little fingers, for chunkier purees that shouldn't be blended but lightly mashed. You can now offer finger foods such as steamed fruits and veggies cut into cubes and watch your baby put the food in his mouth with his own hands.
Make sure to offer only soft foods and watch for choking hazards!

Oats and Melon

Preparation time: 5 minutes
Cooking time: 4 minutes
Servings: 2

Ingredients:

¼ cup Steel-Cut Oats
½ cup diced Melon
½ cup Water
¼ cup Apple Juice

Instructions:

Combine all the ingredients in the Instant Pot. Put the lid on and turn clockwise to seal. When you hear the chiming sound, hit "MANUAL". With the help of "+" and "-" buttons, set the cooking time to 4 minutes. Cook on HIGH pressure.

Press "CANCEL" after the beeping sound. Release the pressure naturally by allowing the valve to drop on its own. Open the lid and fluff the mixture with a fork. Allow to cool before serving.

Store in airtight container in the fridge for three days or freeze for up to three months.

Beef and Tomatoes

Preparation time: 5 minutes

Cooking time: 15 minutes

Servings: 3

Ingredients:

½ cup ground Beef

1 large Tomato, diced

¼ tsp minced Garlic

1 Carrot, finely diced

1 tbsp Olive Oil

⅓ cup Water

Instructions:

Set the Instant Pot to "SAUTE" and add the oil. When hot, add the garlic and cook for 30 seconds. When fragrant, add the beef and cook until it becomes brown. Then stir in the tomatoes and carrots and cook for another 2 minutes. Pour the water over and close the lid. After the chime, set the IP to "MANUAL" and cook on HIGH for 8 minutes.

Press "CANCEL" after the beeping sound. Move the pressure release handle from "Sealing" to "Venting" for a quick pressure release. Open the lid and allow to cool before serving.

Store in airtight container in the fridge for three days or freeze for up to three months.

Creamy Cauliflower Rice

Preparation time: 5 minutes
Cooking time: 2 ½ minutes
Servings: 2

Ingredients:

1 ½ cup Cauliflower Florets

2 tbsp Sour Cream

1 tbsp Ricotta Cheese

Pinch of Turmeric Powder

Pinch of Garlic Powder

1 cup Water

Instructions:

Place the cauliflower florets in a food processor. Pulse until ground and rice-like.

Place the cauliflower rice in the steamer basket. Pour the water into the IP and lower the basket. Put the lid on and turn clockwise to seal. After the chime, hit "MANUAL". With the help of "+" and "-" buttons, set the cooking time to 2 ½ minutes. Cook on HIGH pressure.

Press "CANCEL" after the beeping sound. Move the handle to "Venting" release the pressure quickly, but be careful not to put your hand near the steam. Open the lid and fluff the mixture with a fork. Stir in the remaining ingredients.

Store the leftovers in airtight container in the fridge for three days or freeze for up to three months.

Spaghetti with Dill and Cheese

Preparation time: 5 minutes

Cooking time: 9 minutes

Servings: 2

Ingredients:

2 ounces Spaghetti

1 tbsp Dill

⅓ cup shredded Mozzarella Cheese

1 tbsp Sour Cream

Pinch of Garlic Powder

1 cup Water

Instructions:

Break the spaghetti and place inside the Instant Pot. Pour the water over and put the lid on. Seal by turning it clockwise. When you hear the chime, hit "MANUAL". With the help of "+" and "-" buttons, set the cooking time to 9 minutes. Cook on HIGH pressure.

Press "CANCEL" after the beeping sound. Take the pressure release handle and move it from "Sealing" to "Venting". This will release the pressure quickly. Open the lid and drain the pasta. Meanwhile, whisk the remaining ingredients in a bowl. Place the drained spaghetti inside. Cut them into really small pieces that your baby can handle.

Store in airtight container in the fridge for up to three days. Freezing is not recommended.

Winter Squash in a Veggie Sauce

Preparation time: 10 minutes

Cooking time: 16 minutes

Servings: 4-6

Ingredients:

½ Winter Squash

1 ½ cups Water

1 Carrot, chopped

½ cup Broccoli Florets

¼ cup Mushroom Slices

1 tbsp diced Red Onion

½ Tomato, chopped

1 tbsp Olive Oil

Instructions:

Pour 1 cup of the water into the IP. Place the squash in the steamer basket and lower it into the pot. Close the lid and seal by turning clockwise. When you hear the chiming sound, hit "MANUAL". With the help of "+" and "-" buttons, set the cooking time to 6 minutes. Cook on HIGH pressure.

Press "CANCEL" after the beeping sound. Move the handle to "Venting" and release the pressure quickly. Open the lid and transfer the squash to a cutting board to cool. Discard the cooking liquid.

Wipe the pot clean and add the olive oil. Heat it on "SAUTE". Add the onions and cook for 2 minutes. Then add the mushrooms and cook for another 2 minutes. Stir in the tomatoes and carrots and cook for additional 2 minutes. Add the broccoli and pour the water over. Close the lid. Set the IP to "MANUAL" and cook for 4 minutes on HIGH.

When the screen reads 0:00, move the pressure handle from "Sealing" to "Venting". Open the lid and transfer the veggie mixture to a plate. Mash with a fork but not all the way through. There should be some chunks left.

With a fork and pull off the flesh of the squash to make spaghetti-like strings. Place them in the bowl with the veggies. Cut the spaghetti into pieces your baby can handle.

Store in airtight container in the fridge for three days or freeze for up to three months.

Fruity Bowl

Preparation time: 5 minutes
Cooking time: 5 minutes
Servings: 2

Ingredients:

½ cup diced Pineapple

½ cup diced Apples

1 Apricot, diced

1 Peach, diced

1 Avocado, flesh scooped out

1 tbsp chopped Mint

Pinch of Cinnamon

1 cup Water

¼ cup Apple Juice

Instructions:

Pour the water in the Instant Pot and lower the trivet. In a heatproof bowl, place the pineapple, apples, peach, apricot, mint, cinnamon, and apple juice. Give it a good stir to combine. Place the bowl on the trivet.

Put the lid on the IP and close it by turning clockwise. After you hear the chiming sound, press "STEAM". Set the cooking time to 5 minutes.

Press "CANCEL" after the beeping sound. Release the pressure quickly by positioning the valve to "Venting". Open the lid and remove the bowl from the pot, wearing mittens. Transfer the mixture to a serving bowl. Add the avocado and mash everything, but not all the way through. There should be chunks left. Allow to cool before serving.

Store in airtight container in the fridge for three days or freeze for up to three months.

Shredded Chicken and Brown Rice

Preparation time: 5 minutes
Cooking time: 4 minutes
Servings: 2-3

Ingredients:

¼ cup Brown Rice

½ Boneless and Skinless Chicken Breast

⅓ cup diced Tomatoes

¼ cup Baby Spinach

Pinch of Cumin

Pinch of Garlic Powder

⅔ cup Water

Instructions:

Combine the rice and water in the IP. Then place the lid on top and turn clockwise to seal. When you hear the chiming sound, hit "MANUAL". With the help of "+" and "-" buttons, set the cooking time to 10 minutes. Cook on HIGH.

Press "CANCEL" after the beeping sound. Release the pressure quickly by moving the handle from "Sealing" to "Venting". Open the lid and stir in the chicken, tomatoes, and spices. Close the lid and set the IP to HIGH again. Cook for 12 minutes.

Release the pressure naturally by allowing the float valve to come down on its own. When the valve has dropped, open the lid and stir in the spinach. Put the lid on and seal again. Cook on "MANUAL", on HIGH, for another 3 minutes. Release the pressure quickly and open the lid.

Grab two forks and shred the meat within the pot. If needed, slice the shredded chicken to pieces your baby can handle.

Store in airtight container in the fridge for three days or freeze for up to three months.

Lentils and Turkey

Preparation time: 10 minutes
Cooking time: 13 minutes
Servings: 2

Ingredients:

¼ cup dry Brown Lentils

½ Turkey Breast

Pinch of Turmeric Powder

Pinch of Onion Powder

Instructions:

Combine all the ingredients in the Instant Pot. Put the lid on and turn clockwise to seal. When you hear the chiming sound, hit "MANUAL". With the help of "+" and "-" buttons, set the cooking time to 13 minutes. Cook on HIGH pressure.

When the timer goes off, turn the Instant Pot off by pressing "KEEP WARM / CANCEL". Release the pressure naturally by allowing the valve to drop on its own. Open the lid. Grab two forks and shred the turkey finely within the pot. You may need to slice it if you cannot shred it thinly enough. Stir to combine and allow to cool before serving.

Store in an airtight container in the fridge for three days or freeze for up to three months.

Chunky Mashed Veggies and Yolk

Preparation time: 10 minutes

Cooking time: 8 minutes

Servings: 1-2

Ingredients:

1 Egg

½ Potato, halved

½ Carrot

1 Asparagus Spear

1 tbsp Yogurt

1 tbsp Cream Cheese

1 cup Water

Instructions:

Pour the water into the IP. Place the egg and veggies in the steamer basket and lower it into the pot. Put the lid on and turn clockwise to seal. Select "MANUAL" and set the cooking time to 8 minutes. Cook on HIGH pressure.

Press "CANCEL" after the beeping sound. Release the pressure quickly by positioning the pressure valve to "Venting". Open the lid and remove the steamer basket. Prepare an ice bath and place the egg inside to cool down. When safe to handle, peel the egg and place the yolk in a bowl. Add the remaining veggies and mash with a fork, making sure chunks remain. Stir in the yogurt and cream cheese.

Store in airtight container in the fridge for three days. Not recommended for freezing.

Oat and Flax Apricot Porridge

Preparation time: 5 minutes
Cooking time: 4 minutes
Servings: 4

Ingredients:

½ cup Steel Cut Oats

¼ cup Apricot Juice

½ cup Water

1 Large Apricot, diced

1 tbsp Flaxseed Meal

Instructions:

Combine all the ingredients in the Instant Pot. Put the lid on and turn clockwise to seal. When you hear the chiming sound, hit "MANUAL". With the help of "+" and "-" buttons, set the cooking time to 4 minutes. Cook on HIGH pressure.

Press "CANCEL" after the beeping sound. Release the pressure naturally by allowing the valve to drop on its own. This shouldn't take longer than 10 minutes. Open the lid, fluff with a fork, and stir in the flaxseed meal. Allow to cool before serving.

Store in an airtight container in the fridge for three days or freeze for up to three months.

Steamed Asparagus

Preparation time: 5 minutes
Cooking time: 3 minutes
Servings: 4

Ingredients:

8 Asparagus Spears

¼ tsp Garlic Powder

¼ tsp Onion Powder

1 cup Water

Instructions:

Pour the water into the Instant Pot and lower the rack. Arrange the asparagus spears in a single layer on the rack and sprinkle them with the spices. Put the lid on and turn clockwise to seal. When you hear the chiming sound, hit "STEAM". With the help of "+" and "-" buttons, set the cooking time to 3 minutes.

Press "CANCEL" after the beeping sound. Let the float valve drop on its own for a natural pressure release. Open the lid and remove the asparagus spears from the IP. Cut into small pieces. Allow to cool before serving.

Store in an airtight container in the fridge for three days or freeze for up to three months.

Cheesy Broccoli and Cauliflower

Preparation time: 5 minutes
Cooking time: 3 minutes
Servings: 4

Ingredients:

1 cup Cauliflower Florets

1 cup Broccoli Florets

⅓ cup shredded Cheddar Cheese

Pinch of Garlic Powder

1 tbsp Butter

1 ½ cup Water

Instructions:

Place the cauliflower and broccoli florets in the steamer basket. Pour the water into the IP and lower the basket. Put the lid on and turn clockwise to seal. After the chiming sound, press "STEAM". With the "+" and "-" buttons, set the cooking time to 3 minutes.

When the timer goes off, hit "CANCEL". Release the pressure quickly by moving the handle to "Venting". Open the lid and remove the steamer basket from the pot. Discard the cooking liquid and wipe the pot clean.

Add the butter to the IP and melt it on "SAUTE". Add the steamed veggies and sprinkle with garlic powder and cheese. Cook for a minute or two, or until the cheese is melted. Cut into halves or smaller pieces your baby can handle. Allow to cool before serving.

Store in an airtight container in the fridge for three days or freeze for up to three months.

Buttery Carrot Sticks

Preparation time: 5 minutes
Cooking time: 6 minutes
Servings: 2

Ingredients:

1 Large Carrot, halved and cut into sticks

1 cup Water

1 tbsp Butter

Pinch of Turmeric Powder

Pinch of Onion Powder

Instructions:

Place the carrots inside the steamer basket. Pour the water into the IP and lower the basket. Put the lid on and turn clockwise to seal. When you hear the chiming sound, select "STEAM". With the help of "+" and "-" buttons, set the cooking time to 5 minutes.

Press "CANCEL" after the beeping sound. Position the valve to "Venting" to do a quick pressure release. Open the lid and remove the basket from the pot. Discard the cooking liquid and wipe the IP clean.

Melt the butter on "SAUTE" and add the spices. Place the carrots inside and cook for about 30 seconds or so until well coated with the buttery mixture. Cut into small pieces if needed, and allow to cool before serving.

Store in an airtight container in the fridge for three days or freeze for up to three months.

Long Grain Rice with Tofu and Avocado

Preparation time: 10 minutes
Cooking time: 6 minutes
Servings: 4

Ingredients:

½ cup firm Tofu cut into small chunks

½ Avocado, peeled and cut into small chunks

¼ cup Long-Grain Rice

½ cup Water

1 tsp minced Parsley

Instructions:

Combine the rice and water in the Instant Pot. Put the lid on and turn clockwise to seal. When you hear the chiming sound, hit "MANUAL". With the help of "+" and "-" buttons, set the cooking time to 6 minutes. Cook on HIGH pressure.

Press "CANCEL" after the beeping sound. Release the pressure naturally by allowing the valve to drop on its own. This shouldn't take longer than 10 minutes. Open the lid and fluff the rice with a fork. Transfer to a bowl. Add the remaining ingredients and toss to combine. Allow to cool before serving.

Store in an airtight container in the fridge for three days or freeze for up to three months.

Pumpkin Bites

Preparation time: 5 minutes
Cooking time: 3 ½ minutes
Servings: 2-3

Ingredients:

1 cup small Pumpkin Cubes

Pinch of Nutmeg

Pinch of Cinnamon

1 ½ cups Water

Instructions:

Pour the water into your IP and lower the steamer basket. Dump the pumpkin pieces in the basket and put the lid on. Turn clockwise to seal. Press "STEAM" after the chime. With "+" and "-" buttons, set the cooking time to 3 ½ minutes.

Press "CANCEL" after the beeping sound. Release the pressure quickly by positioning the pressure handle from "Sealing" to "Venting". Open the lid and remove the basket from the pot. Sprinkle with the spices and let cool before serving.

Store in an airtight container in the fridge for 3 days or freeze for up to 3 months.

Rosemary Potato "Fries"

Preparation time: 5 minutes
Cooking time: 15 minutes
Servings: 4

Ingredients:

2 Large Potatoes, sliced

1 ½ tbsp Butter

½ cup low-sodium Chicken Broth

1 Rosemary Sprig

Instructions:

Set your Instant Pot to "SAUTE" and place the butter inside. When melted, add the potatoes. Cook for about 8 minutes, stirring occasionally.

Pour the chicken broth over and put the rosemary sprig inside.

Put the lid on and turn clockwise to seal. When you hear the chiming sound, hit "CANCEL". Then set the IP to "MANUAL". Cook on HIGH pressure for 7 minutes.

Press "CANCEL" after the beeping sound. Release the pressure quickly by setting the handle to "Venting". Open the lid, discard the rosemary, and drain the potatoes.

Place them on a cutting board and cut into small sticks (or pieces) your baby can handle. Serve when cooled completely.

Store in an airtight container in the fridge for three days or freeze for up to three months.

Turmeric Root Veggie Cubes

Preparation time: 5 minutes
Cooking time: 5 minutes
Servings: 3

Ingredients:

⅓ cup Parsnip Cubes

⅓ cup Carrot Slices (or cubes)

⅓ cup Potato Cubes

⅓ cup Rutabaga Cubes

¼ tsp Turmeric Powder

1 ½ cup Water

1 tbsp melted Butter

Instructions:

Pour the water into your IP. Place the veggie cubes in the steamer basket and lower it into the pot. Put the lid on and turn it clockwise to seal. Press "STEAM" after the chime. With "+" and "-" buttons, set the cooking time to 5 minutes.

Press "CANCEL" after the beeping sound. Release the pressure quickly by positioning the handle to "Venting". Open the lid and remove the basket from the pot. Transfer the veggies to a bowl. Whisk together the butter and turmeric and drizzle the root vegetables with it. Store in an airtight container in the fridge for three days or freeze for up to three months.

Cinnamon Pear and Apple

Preparation time: 5 minutes
Cooking time: 3 ½ minutes
Servings: 1

Ingredients:

½ Large Gala Apple, peeled and halved

1 Pear, peeled, cored, and halved

Pinch of Cinnamon

1 cup Water

Instructions:

Pour the water into your IP and lower the steamer basket. Dump the pear and apple into the basket and put the lid on. Turn clockwise to seal. Press "STEAM" after the chime. Set the cooking time to 5 minutes.

Press "CANCEL" after the beeping sound. Release the pressure quickly by moving the handle from "Sealing" to "Venting". Open the lid and remove the basket from the pot. Transfer to a cutting board. Chop into small chunks and sprinkle with cinnamon. Let cool before serving.

Store in an airtight container in the fridge for three days or freeze for up to three months.

Quinoa with Chicken and Peas

Preparation time: 5 minutes
Cooking time: 11 minutes
Servings: 2

Ingredients:

½ cup small Chicken Cubes

¼ cup Quinoa

⅓ cup Green Peas

⅔ cup low-sodium Chicken Broth

1 tbsp Butter

Instructions:

Set the Instant Pot to "SAUTE". Melt the butter in it and add the chicken. Cook until no longer pink. Then stir in the remaining ingredients. Put the lid on and the seal it by turning it clockwise. Press "RICE" after the chime. Set the cooking time to 8 minutes.

Press "CANCEL" after the beeping sound. Make sure the pressure is fully released naturally before opening. The float valve should be all the way down. Open the lid and fluff with a fork. If needed, cut the chicken into even smaller pieces. Serve cooled. Store in an airtight container in the fridge for three days or freeze for up to three months.

Garlic and Parmesan Green Beans

Preparation time: 5 minutes
Cooking time: 3 ½ minutes
Servings: 2

Ingredients:

1 cup Green Beans

1 tbsp grated Parmesan Cheese

1 tbsp Butter

¼ tsp Garlic Powder

1 cup Water

Instructions:

Pour the water into your IP and lower the steamer basket. Dump the green beans into the basket and put the lid on. Turn clockwise to seal. Press "STEAM" after the chime. With "+" and "-" buttons, set the cooking time to 3 ½ minutes.

When the timer goes off, hit "CANCEL". Release the pressure quickly by positioning the pressure handle from "Sealing" to "Venting". Open the lid and remove the basket from the pot. Discard the water and wipe the pot clean.

Place the butter inside the IP and set it to "SAUTE". When melted, add the beans and garlic powder. Cook until well coated. Sprinkle with parmesan cheese. Serve when cooled.

Store in an airtight container in the fridge for three days or freeze for up to three months.

12 – 18 Months

Toddler Meals

Congratulations! You have made it. Your little one can now eat everything you do and whatever the other family members do.

Honey and Cinnamon French Toast

Preparation time: 5 minutes
Cooking time: 15 minutes
Servings: 3

Ingredients:

2 Bread Slices, cut into cubes

1 Egg

1 tbsp Honey

Pinch of Cinnamon

¼ cup Milk

1 cup Water

Instructions:

Pour the water into your IP and lower the trivet. Grease a baking dish with some cooking spray and arrange the bread cubes in it. In a bowl, whisk together the remaining ingredients. Pour this mixture over the bread slices. Place the baking dish on the trivet. Put the lid on and close it by turning it clockwise. Press "MANUAL" after the chiming sound. Using "+" and "-" buttons, set the cooking time to 15 minutes. Cook on HIGH.

Press "CANCEL" after the beeping sound. Release the pressure quickly by positioning the pressure handle from "Sealing" to "Venting". Open the lid and remove the baking dish from the IP. Transfer to a plate and cut into bite-sized pieces. Let cool before serving. Store in an airtight container in the fridge for three days or freeze for up to three months.

Green Feta Egg Cups

Preparation time: 7 minutes

Cooking time: 8 minutes

Servings: 2

Ingredients:

⅓ cup chopped Leafy Greens

2 tbsp chopped Tomatoes, optional

2 Eggs

2 tbsp shredded Cheese

2 tbsp crumbled Feta Cheese

Pinch of Onion Powder

1 cup Water

Instructions:

Pour the water into your IP and lower the rack. Whisk together the eggs and onion powder in a bowl. Stir in the veggies. Take two silicone muffin cups and divide the mixture between them. Place the muffin cups on the rack and put the lid of the IP. Turn clockwise to seal. When you hear the chiming sound, select "MANUAL". Set the cooking time to 8 minutes on HIGH.

Press "CANCEL" after the beeping sound. Release the pressure quickly by positioning the pressure handle from "Sealing" to "Venting". Open the lid and remove the muffins. Let cool before inverting onto a plate. Cut into bite-sized pieces and serve.

Store in an airtight container in the fridge for two to three days. Although you can generally freeze eggs, I do not recommend this method for babies and toddler.

Sweet Potato and Yellow Onion Frittata

Preparation time: 7 minutes

Cooking time: 18 minutes

Servings: 4

Ingredients:

3 Eggs

¼ Yellow Onion, diced

2 tbsp Milk

¼ tsp Garlic Powder

2 tbsp diced Tomatoes

4 ounces shredded Sweet Potatoes

1 tbsp Coconut Flour

1 ½ cups Water

1 tsp Olive Oil

Instructions:

Pour the water into your IP and lower the rack. Grease a small baking dish with the olive oil. In a bowl, whisk together the eggs, milk, and garlic powder. Stir in the remaining ingredients. Pour the mixture into the greased baking dish and place the dish on the lowered rack. Put the lid on and turn it clockwise to seal. Press "MANUAL" after the chime. With "+" and "-" buttons, set the cooking time to 18 minutes. Cook on HIGH.

Press "CANCEL" after the beeping sound. Release the pressure quickly by moving the handle to "Venting". Open the lid and remove the dish from the IP. Let cool before slicing into bite-sized pieces.

Store in an airtight container in the fridge for two to three days. I do not recommend freezing.

Apple and Blackberry Rice Porridge

Preparation time: 7 minutes

Cooking time: 18 minutes

Servings: 4-5

Ingredients:

½ cup Apple Juice

¾ cup Arborio Rice

⅓ cup Blackberries

1 Apple, grated

Pinch of Cinnamon

1 tbsp Butter

1 ½ cups Milk

Instructions:

Melt the butter in the Instant Pot on "SAUTE". Add the rice and cook for about 5 minutes. Add the remaining ingredients and stir well to combine. Put the lid on and turn it clockwise to seal. Press "MANUAL" after the chime. With "+" and "-" buttons, set the cooking time to 10 minutes. Cook on HIGH.

Press "CANCEL" after the beeping sound. Release the pressure naturally by allowing the float valve to drop on its own. Open the lid and give it a good stir. Let cool before serving.

Store in an airtight container in the fridge for two to three days or freeze for up to three months.

Breakfast Cinnamon Bread

Preparation time: 10 minutes

Cooking time: 20 minutes

Servings: 6

Ingredients:

⅓ cup Flour

¼ tbsp Yeast

¼ tsp Cinnamon

1 tbsp Honey

⅓ cup Hot Water

1 tbsp Flaxseed Meal

1 tbsp melted Butter

1 ½ cups Water

Instructions:

Pour the water into your IP and lower the rack. Grease a small baking dish with some cooking spray. In a bowl, whisk together the flour, flaxseed meal, yeast, and cinnamon. Stir in the remaining ingredients. Knead with your hands until a sticky dough is formed. Press the dough into the greased baking dish and place on top of the rack. Put the lid on and turn it clockwise to seal. Press "MANUAL" after the chime. With "+" and "-" buttons, set the cooking time to 20 minutes. Cook on HIGH.

Press "CANCEL" after the beeping sound. Release the pressure quickly by moving the handle to "Venting". Open the lid and remove the dish from the Instant Pot. Let cool before cutting into bite-sized pieces.

Store in an airtight container at room temperature for up to three days or freeze for up to three months.

Mini Mac and Cheese

Preparation time: 5 minutes

Cooking time: 8 minutes

Servings: 2-3 toddler servings

Ingredients:

¾ cup Macaroni

½ cup shredded Mozzarella Cheese

¼ cup Heavy Cream

2 cups Water

Instructions:

Combine the water and macaroni in your Instant Pot. Put the lid on and seal it. You should hear a chiming sound. Select "MANUAL" after the chime. With "+" and "-" buttons, set the cooking time to 5 minutes. Cook on HIGH.

Press "CANCEL" after the screen reads 0:00. Release the pressure quickly by moving the handle to "Venting". Open the lid. Drain the macaroni and transfer to a bowl, but keep the cooking water inside the IP. To the bowl, add the mozzarella and heavy cream and stir to combine. Grease two (or three) ramekins and divide the mixture between them.

Lower the rack into the IP and place the ramekins on it. Close and seal the lid, press "MANUAL" again, and set the cooking time to 2 minutes. Move the handle from "Sealing" to "Venting" for a quick pressure release and open the lid. Serve when cooled.

Store in an airtight container at room temperature for up to three days or freeze for up to three months.

Blueberry Cheesecake Pancake

Preparation time: 10 minutes
Cooking time: 35 minutes
Servings: 4-6

Ingredients:

½ cup Flour

3 tbsp Blueberries

¼ cup Milk

½ cup Cream Cheese, softened

¼ tsp Vanilla

2 small Eggs

2 tbsp Flaxseed Meal

½ tsp Baking Powder

1 tbsp Honey, optional

1 ½ cups Water

Instructions:

Pour the water into your IP and lower the rack. Grease a small baking dish with some cooking spray. In a bowl, whisk together the flour, flaxseed meal, and baking powder. In another bowl, whisk together all the wet ingredients. Combine these two mixtures and be careful not to leave any lumps. Fold in the blueberries. Pour the batter into the greased baking dish and place on top of the rack. Put the lid on and turn it clockwise to seal. Press "MANUAL" after the chime. With "+" and "-" buttons, set the cooking time to 35 minutes. Cook on LOW.

Press "CANCEL" after the beeping sound. Release the pressure quickly by moving the handle to "Venting". Open the lid and remove the dish from the Instant Pot. Let cool before cutting into bite-sized pieces.

Store in the fridge for up to three days or freeze for up to three months.

Creamy and Cheesy Mackerel with Rice

Preparation time: 5 minutes

Cooking time: 7 minutes

Servings: 2-3

Ingredients:

1 Mackerel Filet

2 ounces shredded Cheddar Cheese

1 tbsp Butter

Pinch of Garlic Powder

½ cup Heavy Cream

⅔ cup Cooked Rice

Instructions:

Place your butter in the Instant Pot and set the IP to "SAUTE". When melted, add the mackerel filet and sprinkle with the garlic powder. Cook for two minutes and then flip the filet. Cook for another 2 minutes on the other side. Pour the heavy cream over and put the lid on. Close by turning it clockwise. When sealed, press "MANUAL". With the "+" and "-" buttons, set the cooking time to 3 minutes. Cook on HIGH.

Press "CANCEL" after the beeping sound. Release the pressure quickly by moving the pressure handle to "Venting". Open the lid and transfer to a plate. Cut into bite-sized pieces. Serve with cooked rice.

Store in an airtight container on room temperature for up to three days or freeze for up to three months.

Tomato and Sour Cream Turkey

Preparation time: 10 minutes

Cooking time: 18 minutes

Servings: 3

Ingredients:

1 6-8 ounces Turkey Breast, boneless and skinless

4 ounces diced Tomatoes

⅓ cup Sour Cream

⅔ cup low-sodium Chicken Broth

½ cup cooked Rice

Instructions:

Whisk together the sour cream and broth in the Instant Pot. Stir in the diced tomatoes and place the whole turkey breast inside.

Put the lid on and seal by turning it clockwise. A chiming sound will indicate proper sealing. Select "MANUAL". With the "+" and "-" buttons, set the cooking time to 18 minutes. Cook on HIGH.

Press "CANCEL" after the beeping sound. Release the pressure quickly by moving the pressure handle from "Sealing" to "Venting". Open the lid. Grab two forks and shred the turkey inside the pot. Stir in the rice. Serve when cooled.

Store in an airtight container at room temperature for up to three days. You can freeze the dish, but frozen sour cream gives weird textures to meals, so I do not recommend.

Chicken and Spinach Risotto

Preparation time: 5 minutes

Cooking time: 15 minutes

Servings: 2

Ingredients:

⅓ cup chopped Spinach

⅓ cup small Chicken Cubes

½ cup White Rice

1 tbsp Olive Oil

1 tbsp chopped Onion

¼ tsp minced Garlic

½ cup Water

½ cup Heavy Cream

Instructions:

Place the oil in your Instant Pot and set the IP to "SAUTE". When hot, add the onion and cook for 3 minutes. Then add the garlic and cook until it becomes fragrant, which should take about 30 seconds. Add the chicken and cook until it becomes golden. Stir in the remaining ingredients and put the lid on. Close by turning clockwise. When sealed, press "MANUAL". With the "+" and "-" buttons, set the cooking time to 7 minutes. Cook on HIGH.

Press "CANCEL" after the beeping sound. Let the float valve drop on its own for a natural pressure release. Open the lid and fluff with a fork. Cut into bite-sized pieces. Allow to cool before serving.

Store in an airtight container at room temperature for up to three days or freeze for up to three months.

Breakfast Banana Bread

Preparation time: 10 minutes

Cooking time: 30 minutes

Servings: 4 normal servings and 2 toddler servings

Ingredients:

2 Bananas, mashed

1 cup self-rising Flour

2 tbsp melted Butter

2 tbsp Honey

⅓ cup finely chopped or ground Walnuts

¼ tsp Vanilla Extract

Pinch of Cinnamon

Pinch of Nutmeg

1 ½ cups Water

Instructions:

Pour the water into the Instant Pot and lower the trivet. In a bowl, combine the flour, cinnamon, and nutmeg. In another bowl, whisk together the butter, honey, vanilla, and bananas. Gently combine the two mixtures and fold in the walnuts. Grease a loaf pan or baking dish and pour the batter into it. Place the loaf pan on the trivet.

Put the lid on and turn clockwise to seal. When sealed, press "MANUAL". With the "+" and "-" buttons, set the cooking time to 30 minutes. Cook on HIGH.

Press "CANCEL" after the timer goes off. Move the pressure handle to "Venting" and release the pressure quickly. Open the lid and remove the pan from the IP. Allow to cool before slicing.

Store in an airtight container at room temperature for up to three days or freeze for up to three months.

Bean and Chicken Soup

Preparation time: 10 minutes

Cooking time: 20 minutes

Servings: 4

Ingredients:

½ cup Dried Black Beans

4 ounces Turkey Breasts, chopped

¼ Onion, diced

1 Carrot, peeled

1 Parsnip, peeled

½ tbsp Olive Oil

2 cups low-sodium Chicken Broth

Instructions:

Place the oil in your Instant Pot and set the IP to "SAUTE". When hot, add the onion and cook for 2-3 minutes. Add the rest of the ingredients and give it a good stir to combine. Put the lid on and close it by turning clockwise. When sealed, press "MANUAL". With the "+" and "-" buttons, set the cooking time to 45 minutes. Cook on HIGH.

Press "CANCEL" after the screen reads 0:00. Do a natural pressure release by waiting for the valve to come down on its own. Open the lid and transfer the parsnip and carrots to a cutting board. Cut into small pieces and return to the soup. Serve warm.

Store in an airtight container at room temperature for up to three days or freeze for up to three months.

Beef Patties with Mashed Potatoes

Preparation time: 10 minutes
Cooking time: 20 minutes
Servings: 1

Ingredients:

2 – 2 ½ ounces ground Beef

½ tbsp grated Onion

1 tsp minced Parsley

Pinch of Ground Pepper

Pinch of Paprika

1 tbsp Breadcrumbs

1 ½ tsp Olive Oil

1 cup Water

½ cup mashed Potatoes

Instructions:

In a bowl, place the beef, onion, spices, parsley, and breadcrumbs, Mix with your hand until well combined. Shape into a patty. Place the oil in the Instant Pot and set it to "SAUTE". When hot, add the patty and cook for about 4 minutes per side, or until golden. Meanwhile, grease a baking dish with some cooking spray. Transfer the patty to the baking dish.

Pour the water into the IP and lower the trivet. Place the dish on the trivet and put the lid on the IP. Close by turning clockwise. When sealed, press "MANUAL". With the "+" and "-" buttons, set the cooking time to 7 minutes. Cook on HIGH.

When the timer goes off, press "KEEP WARM / CANCEL". Release the pressure quickly by turning the handle to "Venting". Open the lid and remove the dish from the IP with mittens. Cut into small pieces and combine with the mashed potatoes.

Store in an airtight container at room temperature for up to three days or freeze for up to three months.

Black Bean Hash

Preparation time: 5 minutes

Cooking time: 7 minutes

Servings: 2-3

Ingredients:

1 cup shredded Sweet Potatoes

½ cup canned Black Beans, drained

⅓ cup diced Onion

1 tbsp Olive Oil

¼ tsp minced Garlic

⅓ cup low-sodium Vegetable Broth

Instructions:

Place the oil in your Instant Pot and set the IP to "SAUTE". When hot, add the onions and cook for 3 minutes. Then add the garlic and cook until it becomes fragrant, which should take about 30 seconds. Add the sweet potatoes and pour the broth over. Give it a good stir to combine. Put the lid on the IP and close it by turning clockwise. When sealed, press "MANUAL". With the "+" and "-" buttons, set the cooking time to 3 minutes. Cook on HIGH.

Press "CANCEL" after the timer goes off. Move the pressure handle to "Venting" and release the pressure quickly. Make sure not to put your hand near the steam. Open the lid and transfer to a bowl. Allow to cool before serving. You can serve this topped with sour cream or cream cheese if your baby prefers.

Store in an airtight container at room temperature for up to three days or freeze for up to three months.

Orange Oatmeal

Preparation time: 5 minutes

Cooking time: 4 minutes

Servings: 2

Ingredients:

¼ cup Steel Cut Oats

1 tbsp ground Almonds

1 tbsp Chia Seeds

½ cup Fresh Orange Juice

1 tbsp diced soft Fruit (pineapple, mango, etc.)

¼ Orange, cut into small chunks

Pinch of Cinnamon

1 tbsp Honey

¼ cup Water, for a thinner oatmeal

Instructions:

Place the oats in your Instant Pot. Add the cinnamon, water, and orange juice and stir to combine well. Put the lid on the IP and close it by turning clockwise. After the chiming sound, select "MANUAL". Set the cooking time to 4 minutes and cook on HIGH.

Press "CANCEL" when the screen reads 0:00. Let the float valve come down on its own to release the pressure naturally. Open the lid and transfer to a bowl. Stir in the ground almonds, honey, chia seeds, and fruit. Top with the orange chunks. Allow to cool before serving.

Store in an airtight container at room temperature for up to two days or freeze for up to three months.

Banana Rice Pudding

Preparation time: 5 minutes

Cooking time: 20 minutes

Servings: 4

Ingredients:

½ cup Rice

⅓ cup Heavy Cream

1 Banana, mashed

1 cup Milk

Pinch of Cinnamon

A few drops of Vanilla Extract

1 tbsp Honey

Instructions:

Rinse the rice well under cold water. Pour out the milky water and repeat after the water becomes clean and not cloudy. Place the rice in the Instant Pot. Add the cinnamon, vanilla, honey, and milk. Stir well to combine and put the lid on. Turn it clockwise to close and seal. After the chime, select "PORRIDGE" and set the cooking time to 18-20 minutes.

Press "CANCEL" after the beep. Let the pressure drop naturally by allowing the float valve to come to down position on its own. Open the lid and stir in the cream and banana. Let cool before serving.

Store in an airtight container at room temperature for up to three days or freeze for up to three months.

Kale Quiche with Tomatoes and Olives

Preparation time: 5 minutes

Cooking time: 17 minutes

Servings: 6

Ingredients:

¼ cup Milk

6 Eggs

½ cup diced Tomatoes

¼ cup diced Black Olives

¼ Red Onion, diced

1 cup chopped Kale

¼ cup grated Parmesan Cheese

1 ½ cups Water

Pinch of Garlic Powder

Instructions:

Pour the water into the Instant Pot and lower the trivet. Grease a baking dish and set aside. In a bowl, beat together the eggs, milk, and garlic powder. Stir in the tomatoes, diced onions, olives, and kale. Pour the mixture into the prepared dish. Sprinkle the parmesan cheese over and put the baking dish in top of the trivet. Put the lid on the IP. Turn it clockwise to close and seal. You will know that it is properly sealed when you hear the chime. Select "MANUAL" and set the cooking time to 17 minutes.

After the beeping sound, hit "KEEP WARM / CANCEL". Release the pressure naturally by allowing the float valve to drop on its own. Open the lid and remove the baking dish. Allow to cool before cutting into bite-sized pieces.

Store in an airtight container at room temperature for up to three days or freeze for up to three months.

Breakfast Ricotta Cake with Pears

Preparation time: 5 minutes

Cooking time: 18 minutes

Servings: 4

Ingredients:

1 small Egg

1 Large Pear, peeled and sliced

1 Pear, grated

1 ½ tbsp Olive Oil

½ cup Flour

1 small Egg

½ tsp Baking Soda

1 tsp Baking Powder

¼ tsp Lemon Zest

¼ tsp Vanilla Extract

½ cup Ricotta Cheese

2 tbsp Honey

1 ½ cups Water

1 tsp Butter

Instructions:

Pour the water into the Instant Pot and lower the trivet. Grease a baking dish with the butter and arrange the sliced pear at the bottom. Whisk together the ricotta, egg, vanilla, and honey. Gently whisk in the flour, baking soda, baking powder, and zest. Make sure to get rid of the lumps. Fold in the grated pear. Pour the batter into the dish over the slices pear. Place the dish on top of the trivet and put the lid on the IP. Turn it clockwise to close and seal. Then set the cooking mode to "MANUAL" and cook on HIGH for 18 minutes.

When you hear the beep, press "KEEP WARM / CANCEL". Release the pressure quickly by positioning the handle from "Sealing" to "Venting". Open the lid and remove the baking dish. Allow to cool before slicing into 4 and into bite-sized pieces.

Store in an airtight container at room temperature for up to three days or freeze for up to three months.

Sweet Potato and Spinach Lunch Cakes

Preparation time: 10 minutes
Cooking time: 8 minutes
Servings: 4

Ingredients:

8 ounces Sweet Potatoes, cooked and mashed

⅓ cup chopped Spinach

1 tbsp Sour Cream

1 tbsp Crumbled Feta Cheese

1 tsp minced Parsley

2 tbsp diced Onion

Pinch of Garlic Powder

2 Eggs

1 tbsp Olive Oil

¼ cup Flour

Instructions:

You don't need water for this recipe because you will not be pressure cooking, but sautéing.

In a bowl, whisk together the eggs with the garlic powder, sour cream, and mashed sweet potatoes. Whisk in the flour and get rid of any lumps. Fold in the spinach, feta, parsley, and onion. Shape into 4 cakes.

Set the Instant Pot to "SAUTE" and heat the oil. When hot, add two of the lunch cakes and cook for 3-4 minutes per side, or until golden. Repeat with the other two cakes.

Cut into bite-sized pieces and serve when cooked.

Store in an airtight container at room temperature for up to three days or freeze for up to three months.

18 Months – 3 Years

Family Dinners and Fun Foods

In this category you will find amazing recipes for the whole family that your little one will especially love. Enjoy!

Stuffed Bell Peppers

Preparation time: 10 minutes

Cooking time: 15 minutes

Servings: 3 normal servings and 1-2 toddler servings

Ingredients:

⅔ pound ground Beef

4 large Bell Peppers

½ Yellow Onion, diced

½ cup cooked White Rice

½ cup shredded Cheddar Cheese

⅓ cup Black Beans, mashed

1 tbsp Olive Oil

¼ tsp Garlic Powder

1 ½ cup Water

Instructions:

Add the oil in the Instant Pot and set to "SAUTE". When hot, add the onions and cook for 3 minutes. Add beef and garlic powder and cook the meat until it is brown, about 5 minutes. Transfer the cooked beef and onions to a bowl.

Add the rice, mashed beans, and cheddar to the bowl. Cut the ends of the peppers and deseed. Fill the shallowed peppers with the beef mixture. Put the 'caps' back on the peppers. Pour the water into the IP and lower the rack. Place the peppers on the rack and close the lid by turning it clockwise. Press

"MANUAL". With the "+" and "-" buttons, set the cooking time to 7 minutes. Cook on HIGH.

Press "CANCEL" after the timer goes off. Move the pressure handle to "Venting" and release the pressure quickly. Open the lid and remove the peppers from the IP. Serve when cooled.

Store in an airtight container at room temperature for up to three days or freeze for up to three months.

Spaghetti Bolognese

Preparation time: 5 minutes
Cooking time: 15 minutes
Servings: 2 normal servings and 1 toddler serving

Ingredients:

4 ounces Spaghetti

⅔ pound ground Beef

14 ounces diced canned Tomatoes, undrained

⅓ cup Tomato Sauce

¼ Onion, diced

1 Garlic Clove, diced

Pinch of Oregano

Pinch of Thyme

Pinch of Basil

1 cup Water

Instructions:

Heat the oil in the Instant Pot on "SAUTE". Add onions and cook for 2-3 minutes. Add the garlic and cook for 30 seconds or so, until it becomes fragrant. Then add the beef and cook until it is browned, which should take about 5 minutes. Add the rest of the ingredients to the pot, stir to combine, and put the lid on the

IP. Turn the lid clockwise to seal it properly. When sealed, press "MANUAL". With the "+" and "-" buttons, set the cooking time to 6 minutes. Cook on HIGH.

Press "CANCEL" after the timer goes off. Move the handle to "Venting" to release the pressure quickly. Open the lid and transfer to serving bowls. If needed, cut the spaghetti into smaller pieces for your toddler.

Store in an airtight container at room temperature for up to three days or freeze for up to three months.

Tender Chicken Drumsticks

Preparation time: 5 minutes
Cooking time: 7 minutes
Servings: 2 normal servings and 1 toddler serving

Ingredients:

5 small Chicken Drumsticks

1 tbsp Olive Oil

½ Red Onion, diced

2 cups low-sodium Chicken Broth

3 tbsp Tomato Paste

Pinch of Garlic Powder

2 ¼ cups mashed Potatoes, for serving

Instructions:

Add the oil to your Instant Pot and set to "SAUTE". When hot, add the onions and saute for about 3 minutes. Stir in the tomato paste and garlic powder. Pour the broth over and stir well to combine. Add the chicken and put the lid on the IP. Turn it clockwise to close. When sealed, press "MANUAL". With the "+" and "-" buttons, set the cooking time to 15 minutes. Cook on HIGH.

Press "CANCEL" after the timer goes off. Position the handle to "Venting" and release the pressure quickly. Open the lid and transfer to a bowl. Serve with the mashed potatoes and drizzled with the sauce. If needed, cut the meat from the drumstick in to small pieces for your toddler.

Store in an airtight container at room temperature for up to three days or freeze for up to three months.

Cream Cheese and Spinach Meatloaf

Preparation time: 15 minutes
Cooking time: 25 minutes
Servings: 2 normal servings and 2 toddler servings

Ingredients:

1 Egg

1 pound ground Beef

8 ounces Cream Cheese

½ cup Baby Spinach

3 tbsp Breadcrumbs

½ tsp Rosemary

¼ tsp Onion Powder

¼ tsp Garlic Powder

1 ½ cups Water

Instructions:

Pour the water into the Instant Pot and lower the trivet. Grease a baking dish that can fit into the IP with some cooking spray.

In a bowl, place the beef, egg, breadcrumbs, rosemary, and spices. Mix with your hands to combine well. Lay a piece of parchment paper on a flat surface and spread the meat onto it evenly. In a stripe along the center, spread the cream cheese and top with the baby spinach. Carefully roll the meatloaf into a log, keeping the filling in the center. Place the rolled meatloaf onto the baking dish and place the dish on the trivet.

Put the lid on the IP and close it by turning clockwise. When sealed, press "MANUAL". With the "+" and "-" buttons, set the cooking time to 25 minutes. Cook on HIGH.

Press "CANCEL" after you hear the beeping sound. Move the pressure handle from "Sealing" to "Venting" and release the pressure quickly. Open the lid and transfer to a bowl. Allow to cool before serving.

Store in an airtight container at room temperature for up to three days or freeze for up to three months.

White Pizza

Preparation time: 10 minutes
Cooking time: 7 minutes
Servings: 2 normal servings and 1 toddler serving

Ingredients:

1 store-bought or homemade Pizza Dough

¼ cup Alfredo Sauce

½ cup shredded Mozzarella Cheese

1 ½ cups Water

Instructions:

Pour the water into the Instant Pot and lower the trivet. Grease a baking dish with some cooking spray. Roll out the pizza dough onto a flat, lightly floured surface, then cut in half. Place the halves inside the baking dish. Spread the Alfredo sauce over the dough and top with shredded mozzarella. Put the lid on and turn clockwise to seal. When sealed, press "MANUAL". With the "+" and "-" buttons, set the cooking time to 7 minutes. Cook on HIGH.

Press "CANCEL" after the timer goes off. Move the pressure handle to "Venting" and release the pressure quickly. Open the lid and wait for the pizza to cool to serve.

Store in an airtight container at room temperature for up to three days or freeze for up to three months.

Fun Pink "Meatballs"

Preparation time: 10 minutes

Cooking time: 12 minutes

Servings: 3 normal servings and 1-2 toddler servings

Ingredients:

1 Beetroot, peeled and shredded

1 cup Almond Flour

1 tbsp Olive Oil

1 cup canned Chickpeas, drained

Pinch of Garlic Powder

½ cup Alfredo Sauce

Instructions:

Wear plastic or rubber gloves to avoid staining your hands. Place the beetroot, chickpeas, garlic powder, and almond flour in a bowl. Mix with your hands to combine and shape into meatballs.

Add the oil to your Instant Pot and set the IP to "SAUTE". Place the meatballs inside and cook for about 2-3 minutes per side. Pour the sauce over and put the lid on. Close it by turning clockwise. When sealed, press "MANUAL". With the "+" and "-" buttons, set the cooking time to 6 minutes. Cook on HIGH.

Press "CANCEL" after the timer goes off. Move the pressure handle to "Venting" and release the pressure quickly. Open the lid and serve as desired.

Store in an airtight container at room temperature for up to three days or freeze for up to three months.

Black Bean and Cheese Quesadillas

Preparation time: 5 minutes

Cooking time: 5 minutes

Servings: 4 toddler servings or 1 normal and 2 toddler servings

Ingredients:

2 Whole Wheat Tortillas

¼ cup shredded Cheese

4 tbsp cooked or canned Black Beans

1 tbsp Cream Cheese

3 tbsp Butter

Instructions:

You will not be pressure cooking this, so you don't need water.

Set the IP to "SAUTE" and add half of the butter. When melted, add one tortilla. Spread the cream cheese over and sprinkle with the cheese and beans. Top with the other tortilla and brush the rest of the butter over. After 2 minutes, flip the quesadilla. Cook for another 2 minutes, or until golden.

Transfer to a plate. Divide into quarters and cut one quarter into small pieces. Serve when cooled.

Store in an airtight container in the fridge for three days or freeze for up to three months.

Classic Mac and Cheese

Preparation time: 5 minutes

Cooking time: 8 minutes

Servings: 2 normal servings and 1 toddler serving

Ingredients:

1 ½ cup Water

⅓ cup Milk

2 cups Macaroni

½ tbsp Butter

⅔ cup Heavy Cream

1 cup shredded Monterrey Jack

Instructions:

Combine all the ingredients in the bowl of your Instant Pot. Put the lid on and seal it. You should hear a chiming sound. Select "MANUAL" after the chime. With "+" and "-" buttons, set the cooking time to 8 minutes. Cook on HIGH.

Press "CANCEL" after the beeping sound. Release the pressure quickly by moving the handle to "Venting". Open the lid and transfer to a bowl. Let cool completely before serving.

Store in an airtight container at room temperature for up to three days or freeze for up to three months.

Shredded Pork with Tomatoes

Preparation time: 10 minutes
Cooking time: 95 minutes
Servings: 4 normal servings and 2 toddler servings

Ingredients:

14 ounces diced canned Tomatoes, undrained

2 ¼ pounds Pork Roast

½ cup Tomato Sauce

1 ½ cups low-sodium Chicken Broth

2 tbsp Olive Oil

Instructions:

Add the oil to your Instant Pot and set it to "SAUTE". When hot, add the pork and sear well on all sides. Transfer to a plate and place the remaining ingredients in the IP. Stir well. When combined, return the pork to the pot. Put the lid on and turn clockwise to seal. When sealed, press "MEAT/STEW". With the "+" and "-" buttons, set the cooking time to 90 minutes. Cook on HIGH.

Press "CANCEL" after the timer goes off. Move the pressure handle from "Sealing" to "Venting" and release the pressure quickly. Open the lid and shred the meat inside the pot with 2 forks. Stir to combine well. Serve with rice or potatoes.

Store in an airtight container at room temperature for up to three days or freeze for up to three months.

Salmon Balls

Preparation time: 10 minutes
Cooking time: 8 minutes
Servings: 2 normal servings and 1 toddler serving

Ingredients:

1 ½ can Salmon, flaked and drained

½ Spring Onion, minced

¼ cup Tomato Sauce

½ tbsp chopped Parsley

½ cup Breadcrumbs

½ tbsp Butter

¼ cup Cream Cheese

Pinch of Garlic Powder

1 cup Water

Instructions:

Combine the salmon, onion, breadcrumbs, parsley, garlic powder, and cream cheese in a bowl. Mix well with your hands and shape into small balls.

Place the butter in your Instant Pot and set the IP to "SAUTE". When meted, add the salmon balls and cook until they become golden on all sides, a couple of minutes. Pour the sauce and water over and stir to combine.

Put the lid on and seal it. You should hear a chiming sound. Select "POULTRY", and with "+" and "-" buttons, set the cooking time to 4 minutes.

Press "CANCEL" after the beeping sound. Release the pressure quickly by moving the handle to "Venting". Open the lid. Serve with some mashed potatoes on the side, drizzled with the cooking sauce.

Store in an airtight container at room temperature for up to three days or freeze for up to three months.

Beef and Mushroom Stew

Preparation time: 5 minutes
Cooking time: 22 minutes
Servings: 2 normal servings and 1 toddler serving

Ingredients:

2 Carrots, sliced

2 Potatoes, peeled and cut into chunks

¾ pound Beef, cut into chunks

1 cup sliced Mushrooms

½ Onion, diced

1 tbsp Olive Oil

5 ounces low-sodium Mushroom Golden Soup

6 ounces Water

¼ tsp minced Parsley

Instructions:

Add the oil to your Instant Pot and set it to "SAUTE". Add onion and cook for 3 minutes. When soft, add the beef cubes and cook for a couple of minutes, until the beef turns brown. Add the rest of the ingredients and stir well to combine. Put the lid on and seal it. Select "MANUAL" after the chime. With "+" and "-" buttons, set the cooking time to 15 minutes. Cook on HIGH.

Press "CANCEL" after the screen shows 0:00. Release the pressure naturally by allowing the valve to drop on its own. Open the lid and serve. If needed, cut the beef into even smaller pieces for your toddler.

Store in an airtight container at room temperature for up to three days or freeze for up to three months.

Tomato and Parmesan Tuna Penne

Preparation time: 5 minutes
Cooking time: 3 minutes
Servings: 2 normal servings and 1 toddler serving

Ingredients:

14 ounces canned diced Tomatoes

2 ⅓ cup cooked Pasta

2 cans of Tuna, drained

1 tbsp Olive Oil

½ tsp minced Garlic

¼ cup diced Kalamata Olives

¼ cup grated Parmesan Cheese

Instructions:

Add the oil to your Instant Pot on "SAUTE". When hot, add the garlic and cook for a minute. When fragrant, add all of the remaining ingredients to the pot. Give it a good stir to combine and put the lid on. Turn clockwise to seal. You should hear a chiming sound. Select "MANUAL" and set the cooking time for 2 minutes.

When the timer goes off, turn the IP off by pressing "CANCEL". Release the pressure quickly by moving the handle to "Venting". Open the lid and serve.

Store in an airtight container at room temperature for up to three days or freeze for up to three months.

Mexican Beef Pie

Preparation time: 15 minutes

Cooking time: 12 minutes

Servings: 2 normal servings and 1 toddler serving

Ingredients:

3 Whole Wheat or Corn Tortillas

½ pound Ground Beef

6 ounces shredded Cheddar Cheese

½ cup canned Beans, drained

3 tbsp canned Corn

¼ tsp Smoked Paprika

Pinch of Cumin

Pinch of Garlic Powder

1 ½ cups Water

Instructions:

Pour the water in the Instant Pot and lower the trivet. Grease a baking dish that can fit inside the IP with some cooking spray and set aside.

Place the beef, beans, corn, spices, and 4 ounces of the cheese in a bowl. Stir to combine. Place one tortilla at the bottom of the greased baking dish and top with ½ of the beef mixture. Top with another tortilla and add the remaining filling on top. Place the third tortilla on top and sprinkle with the rest of the cheese. Place the baking dish on the trivet.

Put the lid on and close it by turning clockwise. Select the "MANUAL" cooking mode and set the cooking time for 12 minutes. Cook on HIGH.

When the timer goes off, turn the IP off by pressing "CANCEL". Release the pressure quickly by moving the handle to "Venting". Open the lid and remove the dish from the IP. For the toddler, cut into small pieces.

Store in an airtight container at room temperature for up to three days or freeze for up to three months.

Zucchini Boats

Preparation time: 10 minutes

Cooking time: 13 minutes

Servings: 2 normal servings and 1 toddler serving

Ingredients:

1 Large Zucchini, peeled and halved lengthwis

⅓ cup cooked White Rice

⅓ pound ground Beef

1 Bell Pepper, diced

Pinch of Cumin

Pinch of Garlic Powder

¼ Onion, diced

2 tbsp Tomato Paste

½ cup shredded Cheddar Cheese

1 tbsp Olive Oil

1 ½ cups Water

Instructions:

Add the oil to your Instant Pot on "SAUTE". When hot, add the onions and peppers and cook for 3 minutes. When soft, add the beef and cook until brown, about 4-5 minutes. Stir in the tomato paste and spices and cook for an additional minute. Transfer to a bowl and stir in the white rice.

Pour the water into the IP and lower the rack. Scoop out some of the flesh of the zucchini to make holes to fill with the filling. Divide the beef and rice filling between the zucchini. Sprinkle the cheese on top. Place the zucchini boats on the lowered rack and put the lid on. Seal by turning clockwise and select "MANUAL". Set the cooking time for 5 minutes.

When the timer goes off, turn the IP off by pressing "CANCEL". Release the pressure quickly by moving the handle to "Venting". Open the lid and remove the zucchini boats. Cut into small pieces for your little one and serve.

Store in an airtight container at room temperature for up to three days or freeze for up to three months.

Red Bean Burger Patties

Preparation time: 15 minutes
Cooking time: 20
Servings: 2 normal servings and 1 toddler serving

Ingredients:

1 ½ cup Red Beans, soaked and rinsed

1 cup boiled and mashed Potatoes

¼ cup Panko Breadcrumbs

1 Green Onion, minced

1 tbsp chopped Cilantro

1 Carrot, shredded

1 ½ tbsp Olive Oil

2 ½ cups Water

Instructions:

Pour the water into the Instant Pot and place the beans inside. Put the lid on and turn clockwise to seal. You should hear a chiming sound. Select "MANUAL" and set the cooking time for 15 minutes. Cook on HIGH

When the timer goes off, turn the IP off by pressing "CANCEL". Release the pressure quickly by moving the handle to "Venting". Open the lid, drain the beans, and transfer to a food processor. Discard the cooking liquid.

Place the potatoes, carrots, breadcrumbs, and green onion in the food processor as well. Pulse until well incorporated. Shape the mixture into 1 small and 2 normal burger patties.

Wipe the IP clean and add the oil to it. Set it to "SAUTE". When hot, add the patties and cook until golden on all sides. Serve as desired.

Store in an airtight container at room temperature for up to three days or freeze for up to three months.

Flank Steak Cubes with Broccoli

Preparation time: 10 minutes

Cooking time: 39 minutes

Servings: 2 normal servings and 2 toddler servings

Ingredients:

¾ pound Flank Steak, cut into cubes

⅓ cup Tomato Sauce

½ Onion, diced

8 ounces Frozen Broccoli Florets

⅔ cup low-sodium Beef or Chicken Broth

Instructions:

Place the steak cubes, tomato sauce, onion, and broth in your Instant Pot. Give the mixture a good stir to combine and put the lid on. Turn it clockwise to seal. After the chime, press "MEAT/STEW" and cook on default, which is 35 minutes on HIGH.

When the timer goes off, turn the IP off by pressing "CANCEL". Release the pressure quickly by moving the handle to "Venting". Open the lid and stir in the broccoli. Close and seal the lid again and set the IP to "MANUAL". Cook for only 4 minutes and do a quick pressure release again. Open the lid and cut the beef into smaller pieces for your toddler, if needed.

Store in an airtight container at room temperature for up to three days or freeze for up to three months.

Turkey and Chard Risotto

Preparation time: 5 minutes

Cooking time: 15 minutes

Servings: 3

Ingredients:

1 cup chopped Chard

1 cup small Turkey breast Cubes

1 cup White Rice

1 tbsp Olive Oil

1 tbsp chopped Onion

¼ tsp minced Garlic

½ cup Water

Instructions:

Place the oil in your Instant Pot and set to "SAUTE". When hot, add the onion and cook for 3 minutes. Then add the garlic and cook until it becomes fragrant, which should take about 30 seconds. Add the turkey and cook until golden. Stir in the remaining ingredients and put the lid on. Close by turning clockwise. When sealed, press "MANUAL". With the "+" and "-" buttons, set the cooking time to 10 minutes. Cook on HIGH.

Press "CANCEL" after the beeping sound. Let the float valve drop on its own for a natural pressure release. Open the lid and fluff with a fork. Cut into bite-sized pieces.

Store in an airtight container at room temperature for up to three days or freeze for up to three months.

Turkey and Cauliflower Rice in a White Sauce

Preparation time: 5 minutes

Cooking time: 17 minutes

Servings: 2 normal servings and 1 toddler serving

Ingredients:

12 ounces boneless and skinless Turkey Breasts, chopped

1 cup Heavy Cream

8 ounces Cream Cheese

2 cups Cauliflower Rice (ground cauliflower)

2 tbsp Butter

¼ cup chopped Basil

1 Garlci Clove, minced

Instructions:

Melt the butter in your Instant Pot on "SAUTE". Add the garlic and cook for a minute. When fragrant, whisk in the cream cheese and heavy cream gently. Add the rest of the ingredients and stir well to combine. Put the lid on. To seal, turn it clockwise. You should hear a chiming sound. Select "MANUAL" and set the cooking time for 15 minutes. Cook on HIGH.

When you hear the beeping sound, turn the Instant Pot off by pressing "CANCEL". Release the pressure quickly by moving the handle to "Venting". Open the lid and serve. Cut into smaller bites if needed.

Store in an airtight container at room temperature for up to three days or freeze for up to three months.

Crunchy Macaroni with Tuna

Preparation time: 5 minutes

Cooking time: 10 minutes

Servings: 2 normal servings and 1 toddler serving

Ingredients:

2 ⅓ cups Macaroni

1 cup shredded Cheese

2 cans of Tuna, drained

1 cup of Cream of Chicken Soup

2 tbsp Butter, melted

¼ cup Breadcrumbs

A handful of Crackers, crushed

3 ½ cups Water

Instructions:

Place the macaroni and water in the IP. Put the lid on and seal by turning it clockwise. After the chiming sound, select "MANUAL". Set the cooking time to 8 minutes. Cook on HIGH.

When you hear the beeping sound, turn the Instant Pot off by pressing "CANCEL". Release the pressure quickly by moving the handle to "Venting". Open the lid and drain the pasta. Discard 1 cup of the cooking liquid. Place the pasta in a baking dish and stir in the cheese, tuna, and chicken soup. In another bowl, combine the melted butter and breadcrumbs and sprinkle over the macaroni. Sprinkle the crushed crackers as well.

Lower the trivet and place the dish on top of it. Close and seal the lid. Set the IP to "MANUAL" and cook for 2 minutes on HIGH. Turn the handle to "Venting" for a quick pressure release. Serve.

Store in an airtight container at room temperature for up to three days or freeze for up to three months.

Spaghetti in a Lentil and Sweet Potato Sauce

Preparation time: 5 minutes

Cooking time: 15 minutes

Servings: 2 normal servings and 2 toddler servings

Ingredients:

14 ounces canned diced Tomatoes, undrained

⅓ cup Red Lentils

1 cup Water

1 Sweet Potato, diced

¼ tsp Garlic Powder

8 ounces cooked Spaghetti

Instructions:

Combine the water, tomatoes, lentils, garlic powder, and sweet potato in the Instant Pot. Put the lid on and turn it clockwise until properly sealed, indicated by chiming. Select "MANUAL" and set the cooking time for 13 minutes. Cook on HIGH.

When the timer goes off, turn the Instant Pot off by pressing "CANCEL". Move the pressure release handle to "Venting" for a quick release. Open the lid and stir in the spaghetti. Seal the lid once again and cook on "MANUAL" for another 2 minutes. Move the handle to "Venting" to release the pressure quickly. Open the lid and serve. Cut the spaghetti into smaller strings for the toddler, if needed.

Store in an airtight container at room temperature for up to three days or freeze for up to three months.

Classic Meatballs in a Tomato Sauce

Preparation time: 5 minutes

Cooking time: 8 minutes

Servings: 4 normal servings and 2 toddler serving

Ingredients:

1 ¼ pound Ground Beef

¼ cup Breadcrumbs

1 tsp minced Garlic

½ Onion, grated

1 tsp minced Parsley

Pinch of Cumin

Pinch of Paprika

⅓ cup Tomato Sauce

14 ounces canned diced Tomatoes, undrained

1 tbsp Olive Oil

¼ cup Water

¼ tsp Basil

¼ tsp Oregano

Instructions:

In a bowl, place the beef, spices, parsley, garlic, onion, and breadcrumbs. Mix with your hand until combined and shape the mixture into meatballs. Add the oil to the IP and set it to "SAUTE". Cook the meatballs until they become browned on all sides, for about 5 minutes. Add the water, tomato sauce, and tomatoes and stir to combine. Put the lid on and turn it clockwise. When you hear a chime, hit "MANUAL" and set the cooking time to 10 minutes.

When you hear the beeping sound, turn the Instant Pot off by pressing "KEEP WARM / CANCEL". Release the pressure quickly by moving the handle to "Venting". Open the lid and serve. Store in an airtight container at room temperature for up to three days or freeze for up to three months.

Conclusion

Now that you know exactly what your baby needs to grow into a strong, healthy boy or girl, the next step is to simply blow the dust off your Instant Pot and start preparing these yummy and delicious treats.

Want to know a secret? The purees can satisfy grownups too. Go on, give them a try and you'll see what I am talking about.

CPSIA information can be obtained
at www.ICGtesting.com
Printed in the USA
LVHW05s2311160418
573762LV00003B/44/P